More than just a Birdwatcher

Bob Copping

Published & Printed by Polstead Press
www.polsteadpress.co.uk
info@ghyllhouse.co.uk

Proof copy printed by
THE DOWER HOUSE PRESS

A
Charsidy
Production

ISBN 978-0-9562243-5-4

9 780956 224354

Dedication

To Yvonne for her
understanding
and patience during
my absence.

Best Wishes
Bob Coppinci

Previous books by
Bob Copping

The Tostock Scalliwag   2008

My Years of Pike Fishing   2009

With acknowledgements
to
Nan and David for transcription
and compilation of the book,
my son Adrian
for the 'Descending Ducklings'
and my friend Terry Rednall
for the foreword.

Contents

Contents

Illustrations

Illustrations

FOREWORD

If the readers of this unique book can at least share part of the fascination and excitement of nature that Bob Copping recounts within its pages, then they are in for hours of pleasure.

For more than fifty years I have been more than fortunate in experiencing at first hand the devotion and sheer professionalism of the author. On bird-watching trips we have whispered about waders from dingy wetland hides, plodded amongst plovers over field and meadow, meandered through marshland, strolled over scrub, rambled alongside rivers and foraged through forests in happy pursuit of birds, and also the animals and insects of Suffolk and beyond.

Bob has been an ever-enthusiastic colleague, sharing in my own passion of butterflies and moths, showing an overall interest in a variety of wildlife and excelling in his knowledge of birds. He has noted, photographed and described to the very last detail all his wildlife subjects and his knowledge and enthusiasm can only inspire others to follow in his footsteps.

We regularly meet to discuss, and reflect upon, the creatures that have inspired us, and frequently revisit those special moments from years gone by, when we caught glimpses of the rarer species, also recounting fond memories of the numerous, exciting and pleasurable times that the wildlife of our beloved county has brought us.

It is fitting that a wildlife enthusiast who has put his "all" into his hobby should now have the opportunity to enlighten us with his words.

Terry Rednall

Introduction

I don't profess to be a writer, just an ordinary chap who has always had a love of birds. First, I should make it quite clear that at no time during my photographic recording of nests and their contents, whether from a hide or otherwise, did I put the birds at risk during the most vulnerable stage in their lives. To my knowledge not one deserted their eggs or young through my intrusion.

From a young lad I have always been captivated by finding birds' nests. When discovering certain nests, such as Woodlark, Tree Pipit, Whinchat, etc. I have always derived tremendous pleasure from observing their habitat, nest site, the structure and differing materials used to construct their nests, and then finally seeing the many shapes and colours of their eggs. I must admit that as a young lad I did collect eggs, what we call a schoolboy's collection, one of the few pastimes we had during the war years. Today egg collecting is forbidden and has been illegal for many years. Now I record through the camera lens as many different species as I can find. I have done this since the 1960s.

Before one ventures into this kind of hobby, it's an advantage to know the habitats and behaviour of birds that comes with experience.

The Beginning

From a spring emerging from the ground in the small village of Gedding was the source of the river Rat; many preferred it to be called the River Rattlesden after the village from where it flows. For seven miles it meanders through the countryside, becoming a small river, finally entering the River Gipping at Combs, Stowmarket.

My life started at Rattlesden, a picturesque village very popular with artists. I lived there for six years, during which I cannot remember much of interest happening. To me, birds and creatures were non-existent, not even a Sparrow in the garden. I well remember starting school there, which I thoroughly disliked. Going to and coming from was fine, it was the period between I couldn't come to terms with.

1939 saw the outbreak of WWII and father went into the forces. Soon after, mother, sister and myself moved to Tostock, another pretty village lying midway between Bury St. Edmunds and Stowmarket. At first we moved in with my grandparents who lived in a lovely timbered cottage called 'Oak Cottage'. It has changed very little to this day. Eventually, we moved to Flatts Lane where mother rented a house from the local farmer.

I suppose, typical of old houses in those days, there was no underfelting on the roof so when it rained out came a selection of pots and pans to catch the leaks coming through the ceiling. The plastered walls would bulge through the wet and would have probably fallen off had it not been for the wallpaper.

The garden had eleven different fruit trees, some grass (not lawn), plus an area for vegetables that mother grew. Looking at it now through adult eyes it is hard to believe or imagine how so much was in such a small garden. There was a copper in the outhouse for washing clothes, also a toilet further up the garden with squares of newspaper for toilet paper. Today there is no garden and the house has now been extended and refurbished. We lived there until 1949.

Tostock to me seemed like another world. It was home to the many different birds and creatures that I failed to notice when living at Rattlesden. I soon discovered a wonderful wild and varied habitat, which was called the Tostock Low Meadows; dry during late spring/summer, wet in late autumn/winter. These low meadows started beyond the railway line going right through to the village of Norton.

Running through the Low Meadow was a small, slow congested river called the Blackbourne with dykes running from it dividing it into fields, some of which were lightly grazed by a few cows at certain times of the year. During the winter rains the entire area became flooded. As the floodwater was shallow it only attracted surface-feeding ducks (Dabblers) Mallard, Shoveler and Teal. During spring/summer I would spend countless hours finding nests of Snipe, Lapwing, Moorhen, Pheasant and Partridge, both English and French, taking home there eggs to supplement our meagre wartime rations. If lucky enough to find a duck's nest their eggs were most welcome by mother, as they are very good for baking cakes and buns. Coot and Redshank were not present at this time they came in later years.

Fascination with the varied colours and shapes of these eggs, and the different habitats, started me on the road to a lifelong interest. I frequently visited these low meadows after moving from Tostock, always remembering my young days, especially the smell of the steam trains passing by.

On one such visit during the winter months, a few fields were flooded where I heard the calls of the Teal. I stealthily approached where they were and counted no less than 300. The drakes with their colourful plumage were a treat to my eyes. Teal are our smallest duck; Garganey is almost as small, which we call the summer Teal and comes in small numbers just as a summer visitor. One spring, while searching for other nests: Lapwing, Snipe and Redshank (the Redshank is renowned for being the marsh guard, first to warn other birds of intruders), just by chance I flushed a female Teal from her nest, which contained 9 creamy-white eggs. It is one of the most difficult nests to find. I returned within a week to find the nest/eggs destroyed by a few grazing cows.

Teals nest (not easily found)

* * *

Most times when visiting, I parked my car on the Norton side of the railway bridge. One April morning I was putting on my Wellington boots when I heard the delightful call of the Little Grebe (known as Dabchick) a couple of fields away. I had no idea they were there, not having heard or seen one before, (possibly newcomers). I eventually found the nest, not on the river but in one of the dykes. There wasn't much water and only a sprinkling of reeds. The eggs were covered with vegetation and there was no sign of the birds, which is quite normal for this little bird.

During my wanderings around the meadows, I frequently saw a Kingfisher. I pondered as to where they could be nesting, as the riverbanks were hardly suitable. With binoculars I followed the bird's flight, finding the nest in the earthy roots of a fallen tree. The actual nest chamber was no further than 18 inches from the entrance. I have read they will choose this type of nest site but never encountered one myself.

* * *

The only time I saw geese on these meadows was in the spring of 1971 when the odd White Front would visit. The same year, two pairs of Canada Geese attempted to breed, to my knowledge for the first time, one pair at the Norton end nesting on the riverbank. The second pair made their nest among branches of a fallen dead tree at the Tostock end. Both were happily incubating their eggs. My next visit within a week found both nests had come to grief. Eggs were taken from one nest and cows, I believe, destroyed the other. There was no attempt to breed the following year.

Canada Goose on Nest

* * *

The Low Meadow (marsh) underwent a drastic change after the river was dredged during the 1970s. Large reclaimed areas saw the disappearance of many species of birds, including the winter wild fowl. Many areas of broad-leaved trees were planted. Two lakes were dug to become private carp fisheries. Today, it is unrecognisable.

Before I progress to another chapter of my life, I would like to mention the Kingfisher again.

Kingfisher

For several years I recorded bird sightings, etc., for the annual Suffolk Bird Report. One mission I undertook was counting the nesting numbers of Sand Martins that took me to many disused and working sand pits. One sandpit in question was located at Woolpit; it was a low colony and quite easy to reach to inspect the tunnels with my torch, which I always carried with me.

Whilst doing this I heard the call of a Kingfisher. Within moments, sitting about four feet from me, was the bird with a small fish in its beak waiting to feed its young. I hastily retreated to watch it enter its tunnel, which was among the many Sand Martin holes. This I find is a favourite nesting site for them.

The thing I did find unusual was the distance travelled to get food to feed their young, which I found to be at least half a mile away, from a horse pond on a farm.

The Kingfisher lays about six eggs, often more, and each young bird needs at least twelve fish per day. Imagine the mileage travelled during the youngsters' stay in the nest, which is almost a month, and once they have flown the parents do it all over again as they are double-brooded.

The Kingfisher is renowned for being our most colourful bird. When observed for the first time, one is surprised how small it is, being no larger than a house sparrow.

Many bird books state that they lay their eggs on the bare soil, sand, etc.; perhaps some do, but all the ones I have examined I find that their eggs are laid on a bed of regurgitated pellets (fine fish bones).

I have never read where the feeding male Kingfisher exits the tunnel backwards; I have photographs showing this behaviour. Every pair I have watched feeding their young, the male always does this.

In my opinion the Kingfishers are poor parents. When the young become independent the mortality rate is quite high, either by drowning or starvation.

Incidentally, Ducks and Partridges are the worst parents.

High Minded Mallards

During early spring the low meadows were mostly too wet for the Mallards to nest in their natural nest site. Through experience they knew of a nice dry, cosy and safe nesting place in the hollows of pollarded willow trees alongside the dykes. I would check these whenever possible, finding several nests of 8, 12 and one incomplete clutch of 19 that finished with 21 eggs, the result of two females belonging to one mate. Their normal nesting site on the ground in vegetation is always vulnerable to predators, one such predator being the Carrion Crow. They would steel the eggs of any species found, taking them to a chosen spot to eat, which we call larders. In one such larder I identified the shells from Mallard, Shoveler, Water Hen and, strangely, domestic hen. Hens will on occasion lay away. I have found nests of many eggs, perhaps a broody bird, not far from their home.

Carrion Crow larder

The nearest dwelling from this larder was over a quarter of a mile away. The only other nests I found in these hollows were the incubating Tawny Owls.

* * *

Another time I climbed an isolated dead tree to a Carrion Crow nest some 25 feet high, not knowing at this time it was a nest from the year before. When I put my hand up to feel the contents, a female mallard flew off, at the same time relieving nature all over my head and shoulders (instant camouflage). You can imagine the state I was in. I never wear a hat of any kind but in this case an umbrella would have been more appropriate.

Ducklings in descent

She flew off quacking, or was she laughing, perhaps telling me not to be nosy. She could have flown off much earlier when I started to climb the tree. Probably the eggs (8) were in an advanced state of incubation and she was reluctant to leave until the final moment. Did she do this dirty deed through fright or deliberate like gulls when one enters their nesting colonies?

Usually after my visits I sometimes called at my local public house for a swift half. On this occasion I decided to give it a miss, not being fit to be near anyone.

Leaving School and Onwards

November 1948 saw me leaving school. I had suffered long enough. Twelve months prior I could have left at the age of 14 years but as the education authorities knew I liked it so much they put the school-leaving age up to 15. What luck!

Within a year, my family moved from Tostock to Stowmarket. Both my father and I had employment there. What a relief from cycling back and forth in all weathers. After completing five years' apprenticeship as a carpenter and joiner at O. Seaman & Son, builders, I went straight into the army to do two years' national service, from January 1954 to January 1956 (Suffolk Regiment).

1956 was a busy year for me. I got married, bought a quality caravan to live in, which was situated in the gardens of the Dukes Head Public House – nice and handy for the firm I worked for opposite, and bought my first car, a Morris 8 for £33. I do believe it used more oil than petrol, leaving a smokescreen when negotiating steep inclines. At least I could travel further than I cared to cycle for my bird watching.

Within 2 years, my son was born. The builders for whom I worked at the time decided to make a few redundancies (polite word for sack), owing to the lack of site work during the winter months; I was one of the unlucky ones. I saw an advertisement asking for an estate carpenter at Ringshall Hall. I duly applied for and luckily obtained the job, working there until my old firm crazed me to return as the building work had picked up again. This I did, but I had further plans in mind. My wife and I decided that bringing up a small child in a caravan wasn't a good idea; a Council property would be more suitable. Straightaway I went to the Council and placed my name on the housing list hoping that something would eventually become available. Another part of my plan was now taking shape

At the top of Ringshall hill there was a small thatched cottage belonging to the owner of Ringshall Hall where I worked on the estate. I went to see the owner to ask if he would allow me to rent this cottage. He said that as I had done him a favour when he needed a carpenter he would return the favour by letting me live in the cottage rent-free, providing I reglazed the broken panes of glass behind the boarded up windows. This was wonderful news.

Bob's temporary residence at Ringshall

After collecting the keys, I picked up my wife and son to have the first look inside the cottage. On entering, the first thing I saw in the semi-darkness of the only room downstairs was a little owl, presumably coming down the chimney at some stage and feeding on the many mice that we found living within. After taking the bird's photograph I released it, which I am sure it appreciated. I proceeded to take down the boards from the windows, measured for glass and re-glazed. Once that was done we moved in.

The kitchen had an old range and when lighting the fire for the first time the smoke decided not to go up the chimney, as it was so damp. You couldn't see a hand in front of you. We almost split our sides laughing at that.

When this place was last lived in, goodness knows. The one room upstairs we found was too damp for sleeping in so we made ourselves comfortable in the one room downstairs. Actually, it was quite cosy.

I had a large sectional shed that I erected in the overgrown garden, leaving the end section out so I could park my car under cover. By then I had a Ford Prefect, quite a nice car at that time.

The short time we lived there some of my spare time was taken up walking the woods and fields looking for early birds' nests. I could hardly believe it when I discovered a Song Thrush incubating her eggs in a pile of bramble in my own garden on the 12th February (1961), the earliest recorded ever for Suffolk. At that time Rooks were building and renovating their nests in fruit trees within a walled garden of a large house. These were the lowest rooks' nests I have ever seen, no more than ten feet high. One knows Rooks are communal and many nests form a rookery. Solitary looking Rooks' nests are not Rooks' but Carrion Crows'.

I once climbed to what I thought was a Carrion Crow's nest to find it was a Rook's, the reason being that if for instance a female Rook fails to find a mate she will build a frustration nest away from the rookery, laying and incubating her eggs which are, of course, infertile. During this fruitless period, if she is fortunate to meet up with an unmated male they can then breed as normal in the rookery. No unmated Rook is allowed to build a nest in a rookery; hence the collective noun for Rooks is a "parliament", which they do actually hold.

As I have previously mentioned, there were a number of mice also living with us, rent-free. One evening one came out and sat watching the television, to him a novelty, as it was to us too, as televisions were not that common in those days.

We never, ever saw a rat although every time we visited the outside toilet we would rattle and bang on the boards before we dare enter. Most nights we watched the television with a mousetrap set in the unused brick-floored larder. Two or three mice were caught most nights.

Tawny Owl

Remembering a Tawny Owl's nest I had found in the hollow of a pollarded ash tree just across the field, I decided to take those unfortunate dead mice for this sitting bird incubating four eggs, making sure not to fall over any sheep in the darkness. The Owl would not take the mice from my fingers but would eat the odd one placed in front of her, taking no notice of my torchlight. What the mate thought, goodness knows. He was probably watching my every move from somewhere. I think she looked forward to my nightly visits.

Ever since my boyhood days, I have always found that the place to be during spring/summer was the countryside. Many summer migrants came from Africa to breed and rear families: Nightingale, Black Caps, Garden Warblers are just three and noted as being our three top songsters. Nightingales sing all day and night, becoming mute as soon as their young are born. My wife, son and I were walking through a hazelnut grove one sunny afternoon when I found a Nightingale's nest in a hazel shrub about two feet off the ground. The colour of their eggs is so different to any other British bird, being a dark olive green/brown. It was the finding of this nest that set me on the road to finding and photographically recording the nest and eggs of as many different species as possible. This was a life-long project that took me far and wide. I found Nightingales' nests quite difficult to find even when they are flying back and forth feeding their young. One exception was a nest in a most unusual place in full sunshine in the middle of a track at Northfield Wood, One House near Stowmarket. This nest was built in a deep horses hoof-print; a lovely nest with oak leaves forming a rosette. Owing to its exposed site I don't know whether it survived.

My Plans Realised

I now come to a further chapter in my life.

A vacancy was advertised in the local paper for a carpenter and joiner for the Stowmarket Urban District Council for the maintenance of their Council properties. I applied for this position and was accepted. To me this was a secure position with a regular wage, not having the worry of becoming redundant at any time. Mind you, if the building firm I was working for got to hear I was looking for another job they would have sacked me right away. Their motto, like many other firms, was last in first out regardless of your skills.

This job was a good move in the right direction. I started there, I believe, in the autumn of 1961. There were two other carpenters, and I settled in famously.

Lapwing

While carrying out repairs at the Council Offices I noticed on one door a sign saying "Public Health Inspector". I made time to make an appointment to see the PHI, requesting him to visit the old cottage where we were living. This he agreed to. During his inspection he came down from the bedroom and said 'Do you know there is a pretty bird running about up there?' 'Oh, I am sorry, I forgot to tell you about that'.

I explained to him that I was looking after a Lapwing that was not feeling too well, which I had picked up in the nearby field. It was recovering nicely and would soon be released. He departed after completing his inspection and obviously found the property unsuitable for habitation, especially for bringing up a small child. Not many weeks had passed before the Housing Officer came to see me at work with the wonderful news that a fairly new property had become vacant in Stowmarket. My wife and I were over the moon. My forward planning had fallen into place!

Nest Box Experiences

For 10 years during the 1960s, I made 140 nesting boxes of various designs, erecting them in Gt. Finborough Park near Stowmarket, a large 200-acre park with the small river Rat running through it, a large copse, 17 acres of deciduous trees at the eastern end, and another mixed wood of broadleaf and conifers at the northern end.

I recorded all the occupied boxes during the breeding season, filling in record cards supplied by the British Trust for Ornithology (BTO). These were then returned with all the information required.

I was fortunate in being a carpenter and having access to materials. When renewing floors in properties that had dry rot, a high percentage of these boards were sound and, measuring 6" x 1" thick, they were ideal for my purpose. There were also many off-cuts from the new boards that could be put to the same use. Each completed box was creosoted for weather protection and proved to last well beyond 30 years.

These boxes were inspected once a week during the breeding season, which started late February for Tawny Owls, right through to September when Tree Sparrows decide to have a fourth brood. Tree Sparrows don't start very early; it's rare to find their eggs before 7th May.

After the breeding season, all boxes are cleaned out ready for the winter occupants, and inspected at least three to four times during this period, usually on a moonlit night.

I will now record a few unusual events that I found interesting:

I find my first story amazing. If I had not witnessed this myself it would be hard to believe.

One particular box was occupied by the same pair of Blue Tits year-after-year and recognisable by the above-average clutch of thirteen eggs. They built their nest as usual and were in the process of laying, when a pair of Great Tits decided that they wanted this particular box. The Great Tit is the largest member of the Titmouse family and can be quite pugnacious. They built their nest on top of the Blue Tits' nest where five eggs had already been laid, then proceeded to lay their own normal clutch of eight eggs, which subsequently hatched. At my last visit the young Great Tits were near to flying, a lovely looking family. A week later, doing my usual rounds, I expected to find that they had flown. I opened the box and, sadly, they were all dead.

During the previous week a pair of Tree Sparrows had taken over the box, building their own nest on top of the eight live Great Tits. I noticed something odd in the Tree Sparrows' nesting material, which I extracted to find it was a fully feathered dried carcase of a Wren that they had brought in. The Tree Sparrows went on to rear two broods of their own.

Of the hundreds of nests I studied through those ten years, this was the only example of this behaviour I came across.

When members of the titmice family occupy my boxes (Great, Blue, Marsh and Cole) it is normal practice during the laying period for them to cover their eggs with a soft pad of material made up of fur, hair, feathers and fine mosses, etc. Each morning they return to the box to lay a single egg, uncovering and covering up the eggs until the final egg is laid. She then sits and incubates full time.

During this laying period when the nest is undisturbed during the day, I have often come across a type of bumblebee that has entered the box and buried itself in the egg covering-pad, making a waxy yellow/orange sticky object about the size of a marble. When disturbed, the bee creates much buzzing. When the rightful occupier returns to lay another egg, she encounters this buzzing and deserts the box immediately. Obviously, when this unfortunately occurs it disrupts her laying sequence and a new home has to be found – another nest box perhaps? This could account for my occasionally coming across a solitary egg on the bare base of a box

The new owners (Great Tits mostly) would build their nests hurriedly, bringing the eggs up to the finished nest and carry on as normal.

* * *

One particular nest box was occupied by Great Tits. When I inspected it, it revealed five eggs plus three quite large acorns, which she happily incubated. I assume she could feel those acorns below in the nesting material mistaking them for eggs and bringing them up into the clutch.

Eight eggs were her normal amount – why not eight eggs plus acorns?

You may wonder how the acorns got into the box; they were left by the mice that inhabited the box during the winter months.

* * *

Starling nestbox with eggs

Tree Sparrow's nest and egg

Great Tit emerging from nest box.

Blue Tit at box

I now come to a larger bird occupying a few boxes: the Jackdaw

I found they regularly laid their eggs around the 17th-19th April, having one brood a year, as does the rest of the Crow family. In this particular box, I remember the pair rearing one young as opposed to the normal four. Once the young had flown, I still continued to inspect the boxes, knowing that through the years Stock Doves could occupy them.

One week after this single young Jackdaw had flown, I looked into what I thought was going to be an empty box so I was much surprised to find eight or nine golf balls. I had previously seen a Jackdaw carrying a golf ball from the nearby course a few hundred yards away. I removed the golf balls from the nest box. At that time, in the mid 1960s, the course was only nine holes. On my rounds I would collect the lost golf balls to sell on to my golfing friends. When I visited this box the following week a Stock Dove (country name Blue Rock) flew out. It had laid their usual two eggs, and went on to successfully rear two young.

There were no Grey Squirrels in the park in the early 1960s, only Red. That was to reverse very soon when all the larger boxes were taken over by the Greys.

During my interesting 10 years of nest-box surveying, there were times when the occupants were present, either in the process of laying, incubating or brooding their young. I would take the bird off its nest, count either the number of eggs or young then replace it. Most times it would remain in the box. This only applied to the Titmice and, on occasion, Tawny Owls. I can honestly say in all my years no nest was forsaken by my intrusion.

* * *

There were two creatures that disrupted my records. Firstly, the weasel (country name mousehunt), a lovely little creature and a prolific predator. They would enter a nest box, probably attracted by the begging calls of the young within, and devour them all; they were mostly Great and Blue Tits.

The weasel can quite easily get through a wedding ring. A 1" hole in a nest box was not a problem.

* * *

The other creature was the Great Spotted Woodpecker, which would hammer a hole anywhere around the nest box, not necessarily at the main entrance, to gain entry and eat the young of Blue and Great Tits. This Woodpecker is well-known for this activity.

As the winter and dark nights approached, I made sure that all the boxes were cleaned out ready for the incoming winter residents. The first few years during the 1960s I had Red Squirrels occupying boxes (3 in one box). A few years later they were pushed out by the Greys. Mice took over quite a few boxes, some making a nest, others using them for larders, bringing in acorns mostly and a few hazelnuts. One box I opened was full of conkers (or horse chestnuts). This was during dark hours. I returned to this box during the day and counted over 40 conkers. Thinking perhaps someone was playing a practical joke, I checked every conker to see if they all went through the 1" aperture, to my surprise they did. How many times did this mouse encounter one not passing through?

A few different species of bird used my boxes for sleeping quarters. They were, in order of numbers – Great and Blue Tits, Tree Sparrows, Starlings, a solitary Nuthatch, plus a solitary Great Spotted Woodpecker, which remained in the box before and after it was photographed. Unfortunately, I found the Nuthatch dead on my next visit.

When the nesting season began in the spring a pair of Nuthatches started to nest in this particular box. Materials for the so-called nest were brought in: larch/pine chippings and a few small dead leaves on which to lay their eggs. Nuthatches have the habit of reducing the entrance hole with mud to suit their body size. In this case there was no need, as the aperture was just one inch already. They must have felt the need to mud somewhere for, although the box was draught-proof, they put a mud sealant around the inside of the removable lid, as seen in the photograph on page 23. To my disappointment they didn't lay their eggs owing to a pair of Tree Sparrows taking over the box.

If Tree Sparrows want a box they will move in regardless of any other resident, they are notorious for this.

All in all, the 10 years' survey of my boxes was a very busy and interesting period. Not so much all the tree climbing keeping me fit but the many other projects I had on the go, also relating to birds, which you will read in other stories.

Postscript

Of all the thousands of eggs I saw over the 10 years, I only ever found 4 runts. These runts are miniature and identical eggs to the normal size but have no yoke; two were of Great Tits, the other two Blue Tits.

Nature Reserve

Great Finborough Hall (a mansion) built in 1795 of white brick stands in 200 acres of parkland. Through my nestbox period, it was owned by the Eastern Electricity Board.

In the early 1970s, the committee of the Stowmarket Naturalists Society received a letter from the E.E.B. asking if we would like to attend a meeting at the Hall to discuss a proposition that could be of interest to us. The date and time were arranged and at this meeting the E.E.B. officials asked us if we would like to undertake seventeen acres of woodland as a nature reserve at a peppercorn rent of £1 per year. Within these seventeen acres was the old gamekeeper's cottage. Sam Francis was the gamekeeper, who became a good friend of mine through the years.

I met Sam one morning down by the river. He greeted me saying 'Morning, Bob. Oi sin suffin oi int sin afore' 'What's that', I replied. He answered, 'It's one of them cowpies'. 'You mean a coypu'. 'Yes, one of them as well', he said. I had to chuckle.

The cottage had been empty since his retirement, maybe before, and was reached by crossing the river bridge. I knew the proposed area well from my previous nestbox days; there were breeding Kingfishers, Grey Wagtails (at the weir) and all the many woodland birds.

After much discussion, the E.E.B. officials left the room to enable us to mull over the offer and to decide one way or another. Would you believe that our members were not of a mind to take this on! I must admit I got a bit distraught with them.

I forgot to mention that I also was a committee member. I put it to them that all the time I had been a member of the S.N.S., which was several years, they had done nothing and were quite happy to be led by people like me telling them this was a good opportunity to do something worthwhile. In the end they came round to my way of thinking and agreed.

I was made one of the trustees. As with most clubs and societies there is always the shouters and the doers; I was, without doubt, a doer. A week or two later a few others and I were invited to the Hall for a posh meal along with other high-ranking officials, plus the media for the official handing-over of this nature reserve. Everything went very well and it was now down to us to make it successful.

First, the gamekeeper's cottage (which needed quite a bit done to it), was to become a study centre. I, being a carpenter, repaired the leaking roof, the windows and doors plus whatever my skills required. Other members did decorating and odd jobs.

The ornamental brickwork on the bridge leading to the study centre had been vandalised through the years and finished up in the river. This had to be made safe for the forthcoming visitors. My friend, Terry, assisted me in this project, cutting down tall and slender trees from the north wood to make a rustic barrier. I must admit the finished work looked very good.

My next project was to collect several of my nesting boxes from the eight-hole golf course area. These had to be repaired, mainly from woodpecker damage, creosoted and erected around the reserve to supplement those already established.

The cottage (study centre) had no electrical or water supply at this time. The E.E.B. agreed to bring these services, which was quite a distance. Everything seemed to be going very well. We had many visitors, busloads of school children and naturalist parties. I used to lead the bird enthusiasts around the reserve hardly ever failing to see Kingfisher and Grey Wagtails, a treat for many people.

This went on, I suppose, for at least a year, when out of the blue the committee received a letter from the E.E.B. stating that from such a date we could no longer have this nature reserve. I didn't know at that time the particular reason for the turnaround. Obviously we were all at a loss having put in so much time and effort with the project; but there was nothing we could do.

We set about clearing the study centre of exhibits, the many photographs showing birds at and in my nest boxes, also my collection of nests of the smaller birds that I accumulated through the years and were of tremendous interest to children and adults alike. They went on to be given to the Bramford Primary School. Our nature reserve soon became a thing of the past, enjoyable while it lasted.

A few years later the nine-hole golf course was extended to eighteen. The cottage (study centre) was fully modernised to become a holiday dwelling. We all felt the E.E.B. really wasn't very kind to us. Did they know what was to come when they first approached us?

In my opinion Grey Squirrels are the most undesirable creatures ever to be introduced into this country. When they invaded our nature reserve during the 1960s, the nesting success of smaller birds took a drastic toll; eggs and small young were eaten wholesale.

Hole-nesting birds were safe if the apertures were too small for this menace to enter. Starling nest boxes suffered, as the entrance holes were one-and-a-half inches in diameter and many young were eaten.

We sought expert advice, hoping to eradicate these pests only to be advised that it would be a waste of time. It was explained to us that if there were twelve pairs in the reserve and these were disposed of, twelve more pairs would move in to take their place. It's as well to accept what numbers you already have. To give one example of these destructive creatures:

Long Tailed Tit at Nest

I kept regular observations on a pair of Long Tailed Tits building their nest in a bramble bush. Their nests are one of the most beautiful of all British Birds, taking up to three weeks to complete. Starting in March, they work continuously on the main outside structure collecting lichen, mosses and spiders' webs. The actual nest is shaped like a bottle with the entrance near the top (country name Bottle Tit).

Once the outside is complete, they take a deserved break from building. Later they set about completing the nest, lining the inside with feathers. It is then ready for them to lay anything up to a dozen eggs.

These tiny, pretty little birds were incubating their eggs for a period of time when along came a Grey Squirrel and destroyed the nest, eating the eggs, or any small young. At least six weeks of labour all in vain.

Long tailed Tit nest

To give you an idea of the work involved making one of these nests, not counting the materials used for the main structure, I dissected six nests and found one nest containing 2,184 feathers, which had been collected singly. I have watched them frantically trying to separate feathers, before putting them in position. Sometimes I have watched them dismantling a complete nest they have built to rebuild it somewhere else.

Their nests are easy to find, no higher than six feet from the ground, rarely higher, with the entrance usually facing the sun. I find blackthorn and gorse bushes most likely nest sites but there are many others: bramble, dog rose, etc.

The only credit I give the Grey Squirrel is that they possess a wonderful brain!

That's Fighting Talk

Bordering the River Gipping at Baylham were several privately owned, worked-out gravel pits: 2 large and several small ones. A friend, whom I worked with at Stowmarket during the 60s, knew I was a keen birdwatcher. He told me that there were some Little Grebes nesting there. Before I ventured to the area, I wrote for permission to the owner, a Miss Eastall who lived at Haughley. She kindly gave me right of way.

Little Grebe's nest and eggs

After an enjoyable look around one afternoon, during which time I saw 3 pairs of Little Grebes plus numerous other birds, I headed back to where my car was parked. I saw in the distance a chap standing on the top of a heap of ballast waving his fist at me. I waved back and carried on walking towards him. As I approached him, he put up his fists saying that I could have it rough if I liked. I asked him what on earth he was talking about, telling him I had permission from the owner to be there. He asked me who that might be and I told him. He said that, in fact, the land didn't belong to her; it was the other pit system. After explaining my presence, he simmered down. From that day we became great friends. He was a lorry driver for the firm that owned the property. He and his good wife lived in a caravan on site. When not at work he kept an eye on the site. I frequently visited there, usually stopping at their caravan for a chat over a cuppa.

The Gipping Valley was extensively excavated for sand and gravel (still is to this day) leaving large sheets of water to become leisure areas for anglers, birdwatchers and walking nature-lovers. In 1972 preparations for the A14 (which was the A45) were in progress. The Little Grebe nesting sites were doomed, as the smaller pits on which they nested were filled in with a massive tonnage of fly ash, I assume from the Ipswich power station. From then on I don't think these charming little diving birds have since nested in the valley. The remaining larger pits are not suitable for them, as they prefer small shallower waters as opposed to larger ones, which the Great Crested Grebes prefer. Many pairs regularly nest along the valley.

***

When all the grey fly ash was brought to this site some of the heaps became consolidated. I found Sand Martins nesting in them. I have a photograph of a Sand Martin sitting on her nest – how unusual is that?

Canada Geese first nested in the valley in the early 1960s. Now they occupy the many gravel pit islands, nesting safely from predators, there number increasing yearly. Grey Lag Geese, a latecomer to the valley in recent years, are also increasing. Last autumn (2009) I estimated 500 Geese grazing at their regular spot at Baylham; two-thirds of them were Canada Geese.

Egyptian Geese

The most recent goose to appear in the valley over the past twelve months is the Egyptian. Mostly seen at the Station Lake, Needham Market and the Causeway Lake at Baylham. A colourful and welcome addition to the valley's wildfowl.

One bird that has taken up residence in the valley is the Cormorant. The angling fraternity has named them "the black death", as they do untold damage to fisheries, eating large quantities of fish daily. One cannot fail to notice these large black birds sitting with open-stretched wings drying their feathers, as they have no waterproofing like other wild fowl. Sometimes they are so full of food they have difficulty taking wing. Being local to me, I have visited the Gipping Valley for over 50 years. It has such a varied wild life, never knowing what one will see during any month of the year.

Apart from Great Grey Shrike, Osprey, and Smew, I suppose the rarest sighting was of a party of Bearded Tits at Barham in a reed-bordered pit one sunny morning.

A bird that is commonly seen is the Little Egret, now a familiar sight flying up and down the valley. It is only a matter of time before this nice little bird sets up a nesting colony inland.

Get yourself out walking the valley river path, you never know what delights you will see.

Belfry Jackdaw

I am not a religious person, but during the eleven years I worked for the Stowmarket Urban District Council, I went to church two times a week, on Monday and Friday, to wind the clock at St. Peter and Mary Church. I was asked to do this on a voluntary basis, which I accepted. As the Suffolk saying goes: "Suffolk born, Suffolk bred, strong in the arm and weak in the head". I don't know whether the latter is applicable. You had to be strong in the arm and I was advised not to undertake winding after a meal. This, of course, gave me access to the belfry and spire during birds' breeding season. The only birds I found breeding there were quite a few jackdaws, which entered through the louvred Gothic windows, bringing in loads of sticks for their nests. In enclosed nesting sites, such as nestboxes and small hollows in trees, hardly any sticks are used. During the 1960s the bells were taken away to be retuned. When the belfry became empty of bells all the masses of sticks that had accumulated through the years were removed, after which they put wire netting over the windows to prevent this happening again. When the bells were re-hung, the jackdaws could still nest between the louvres minus sticks. One mid-April a jackdaw's nest containing four eggs was there for me to photograph.

The next clock-winding session saw me with pliers, hammer and camera. As I didn't wish to have a photograph with netting in front, I unpinned it and bent it down. Photo taken, off I went on my cycle to wherever I was working in the town. About two hours later it dawned on me that I hadn't replaced the netting at the nest. Back I went, up the stairs, opened the belfry trapdoor to find no less than a dozen jackdaws that had found their way through the small hole. I wondered how on earth I was going to get rid of them. I opened the next trapdoor, which led to the outside beneath the spire; it is the only thing I could come up with. Back to work once again, returning late afternoon. To my surprise, and relief, all the jackdaws had gone through the open trapdoor. All I had to do then was shut the trapdoor, nail the netting back to the window and go home. Panic over!

Jackdaw nest in Belfry

I will carry on later with a jackdaw story, but first, as I am dealing with the church, I will tell you another story concerning Rooks.

From the top of the church, one has a panoramic view of the town. On one side one overlooked a rookery. At that time there were many nests, today perhaps a couple. May 12th is an official rook-shooting day, although today they no longer shoot. This rookery was never included, as it was situated in the town centre. The reason the 12th May was decided is at that time the young Rooks, called branches, could not actually fly but would spend a lot of their time on the perimeter of their nest exercising their wings ready for when they take their first flight. Some will venture a little further from their nests, which can be their downfall. Downfall is the right word, as some unfortunates finish up on the ground beneath the rookery. Once grounded the parents disown them, they will not feed them, they are destined to die. I, being a good Samaritan, would collect these young rooks, take them to the top of the church and release them towards the trees below. They would, hopefully, crash into the branches and get a foothold where they could be fed by their parents.

Rooks build their nests with live twigs, broken with their beaks from trees. Many twigs fall to the ground, but they will not go down and pick them up because they risk picking up dead ones. There are only two types of stick that make a Rooks nest: bent ones and straight ones.

Back to the jackdaws, which I mentioned earlier. Nosing about among the jackdaw nests it was surprising to see quite a few pieces of silver paper, foil, etc. It is a known fact that jackdaws are attracted to shiny objects. The town's streets provided them with many. I first discovered this when I was a boy living at Tostock. I was the only boy in the village to rear a jackdaw. I first got it out of the tree hollow at a very early stage. I called it Jack, which he would respond to. He became a true friend, coming with me everywhere, perched on my left shoulder. I found he liked shiny objects, especially when he used to bring me sixpences left as change by the milkman on people's doorsteps. That was a secret between Jack and me.

Sunday was the only day of the week that the milkman didn't deliver to the door. Instead he would come to the forecourt of the Gardeners Arms public house and ladle out the milk into the villagers jugs. Sister and I would take it in turns every Sunday to collect the milk. This particular Sunday was my turn, armed with my jug, Jack on my shoulder plus half a crown to pay for the milk; I did of course get change. Whilst waiting for the milkman to arrive, I was sitting on the wooden enclosure that protected the chestnut tree; this tree was planted in 1935 to commemorate the Silver Jubilee of King George V and was just a sapling in those days, today a splendid tree. Inside this enclosure was a mixture of long grass and nettles. I had one of my silly brainwaves by offering my half-crown piece to Jack sitting on my shoulder. Immediately it snatched the coin. That was when I panicked, knocking my in-flight Jack into the nettles. Jack flew off unhurt, dropping the coin somewhere in the rough. By then the milkman had arrived and was serving out the milk. By the time I found the money, the milkman was about to leave. I did get my milk, what a relief, father wouldn't have been too pleased if I had gone home without it.

Studies of Starling Roosts

It was not until the early sixties that I decided to study in detail the starlings' roosting habits and behaviour in Suffolk. My fascination for this most successful species in the modern world started one winter's evening whilst observing thousands of these birds winging their way towards their nightly roosting place. I later found this to be at Little London, near Stowmarket. This roosting place was called Bushy Meadow, four acres of hawthorn bordered by larger broad-leaved trees and surrounded by arable land. The first record I have of this place goes back to 1960 when the numbers were then approximately seven thousand. This built up through the forthcoming years to one million birds in 1974-5.

The first of these migratory birds arrive probably late September or early October, the bulk arriving throughout October and November, coming mainly from the Continent and Denmark, though I have records of birds from as far away as the U.S.S.R. and North Norway. These records were obtained from the many ringing cards submitted to me by the Suffolk ringers and also by rings, which I have found on dead, and dying birds beneath their roosting places. The first place they roosted on arrival in Suffolk was at Westhorpe, approximately eight miles from Stowmarket, in fifteen acres of hawthorn, a similar situation as the Little London roost. They would stay at Westhorpe until late November when they moved to Little London, leaving behind other species of birds that also used to roost, i.e. members of the Thrush family and Finches, and the odd Budgerigar which foraged by day with a flock of House Sparrows but roosted at night with Tree Sparrows. The Starlings would then stay at the Little London site for the rest of the winter, departing for their breeding quarters from late February-March onwards.

To count these vast numbers of birds has to be done, in my opinion, in the morning when all the birds are known to be present and have not left for their favourite feeding areas, which could be as far away as thirty miles from a roost. To count incoming birds at night proves difficult as several stragglers arrive during darkness. I usually get to a roost around 6 a.m., climb a tree overlooking the whole area and await their methodical departure just after first light. The first large wave of birds will fly off to all points of the compass, then every five minutes further waves will take off until the roost becomes silent. These waves are approximately the same strength, so if one can ascertain the strength of one wave and multiply it by the number of waves that have left the roost, then an approximate number of birds in a given roost can be estimated. The only remaining birds are the dead and dying, and the predators that these roosts attract. These remaining birds, which are fairly active but mostly flightless, band together during daylight hours.

There have always been many puzzling things regarding the roosting behaviour of Starlings. They obviously converse with each other somehow; otherwise how is it that when they depart from a roost in the morning none returns at night but all arrive at another spot?

Whilst inspecting the floor of one roost, which I did regularly, my eyes set upon many elastic bands of all shapes and sizes. Many more hung from the lower branches. These had obviously been picked up and eaten by the birds in mistake for earthworms, which at a glance they resemble, and the Starling, notorious for its greediness, cannot take chances. During the night their digestive juices go to work with the result that the bands are regurgitated with other indigestible matter. These elastic bands are picked up in great numbers mainly at refuse tips, especially with today's modern packaging methods. On looking further I have also found many in the gutters in towns.

It was on the morning of 4th January 1969 that I noticed some strange objects in one particular area of a roost. These objects were yellow and grey and about three quarters of an inch long. I gathered up 344 of these. As many as 750 were present but were not accessible. Inside these small sac-type objects were small particles of food, grit and juices. I took samples of these to the local vet who then asked if I could obtain half a dozen fresh dead birds from the roost. I did this the next morning and the result was that these objects were in fact gizzard linings of the Starlings. All the specimen Starlings had theirs intact. Specimens of these gizzard linings were sent to Cambridge University but to my knowledge no light has been shed on the situation; it will probably remain an ornithological mystery. The linings were not the distasteful piece left over from being eaten by a predator, as too many appeared too quickly. The mortality in a roost of three quarters of a million birds is roughly two-dozen birds a night. These gizzards appeared just as the weather worsened to snow and continued only throughout January; I have not encountered them since. The feeding area of that particular roosting party would perhaps have been helpful.

On one particular occasion, after torrential rain, masses of earthworms lay dead on top of the inches-thick bird droppings, dead through the ammonia washing into the ground. These were the largest worms I have ever seen, and remained untouched by the birds.

I wondered perhaps if these birds roosted together for warmth, so I put up minimum-maximum thermometers inside and outside the roosts. Surprisingly, each time there were no differences, although it felt vastly different to the human body.

Gizzard Linings

As the Little London roost was in a direct flight line with R.A.F. Wattisham (which was two miles distant), I wrote to, and was kindly granted permission by, the Station Commander to watch the incoming planes at the crucial moment when the Starlings were flighting in, to compare height, speed and danger of airstrike. All these factors could be seen on the radar scanning panels housed in the control tower.

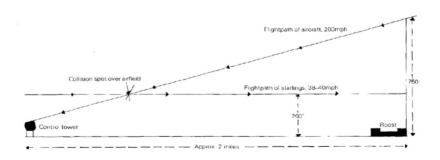

Starling flight path calculations

That particular evening the Starlings were homing in at 200 feet. The planes' height over the actual roost was 750 feet and their speed was 200 m.p.h. Collision point that evening was three quarters of a mile from the control tower. The height of incoming Starlings varied with weather conditions. Incidentally, Starlings fly each night from their feeding ground to their roosts in a direct A to B line at 38-40 m.p.h. (checked for miles by car) picking up small feeding parties en route. On reaching the vicinity of the roost, flocks, or rather murmurations, the birds numbered tens of thousands.

During late 1968, for a short period, I traced nearly all the Suffolk Starlings to Thorpe Abbot, just over the border into Norfolk. They were roosting there in what was called The Grove. I estimated two million birds there. This roosting place was all out of character as the wood was mostly ash, whereas all the Suffolk ones I have covered have been hawthorn. The Thorpe Abbot site has since been deserted.

It was not until the early seventies that the roosting pattern completely changed, owing to the roosts at Westhorpe and Little London being reclaimed for agricultural purposes. The birds then appeared at a disused overgrown sandpit at Norton where I estimated one million birds. They returned there for a further two winters before separating into several smaller roosts throughout the county. The landowners have tried to discourage them by shooting but with no success. To sit in the middle of a large roost in a hide is quite an experience, as they assemble on every branch and twig only pecking distance from each other. Their incessant squabbling and chattering continue all night long. They readily accept photographs being taken with an electric flashgun at close quarters and the emergence of oneself from the hide, but switching on a torch causes immediate panic. When their departure time has come, I cannot but wonder if these interesting birds will return in even greater numbers the next year to delight the ornithologist with their wonderful aerial manoeuvres, which they perform prior to going to roost; quite a sight to be seen.

Postscript

There were two albino Starlings that came to roost, sitting beside each other in the same place every night.

I placed an article in the local paper asking if anyone had seen either of these two birds feeding in their garden. A reply came from a woman in Kesgrave, near Ipswich, who had seen one in her garden. Kesgrave is eighteen miles from the roost at Westhorpe as the Starlings fly.

Television Debut

I was a regular member of the "Stowmarket Naturalists Society" and was now able to walk to the monthly meetings, which were then held in the Middle School. At one of these meetings it was announced that a TV cameraman, named Doug Fisher, was shortly coming to live at Upper Combs, a couple of miles out of town. Once Doug and his family had settled into their new home, he invited us naturalists to his studios to see a film, which he had made on Gannets and other seabird colonies on the Island of Grassholm, six miles off the Welsh coast, and a very entertaining evening was had by all. I remember being asked by our chairman to give a vote of thanks, but being so shy I had to decline.

Later, he put out feelers as to who was the local know-it-all regarding natural history, mainly birds, and all avenues led to me. I later received an invitation to visit his home for a meal and general chinwag. I felt privileged and got a little excited having been asked. Late one Saturday afternoon off I went as arranged. On arrival he introduced me to his wife, two boys and a thoroughly spoiled shorthaired dachshund, named Cleo. During my visit he explained that he was in the process of making a series of thirteen films entitled "Another World" for Granada/Anglia Television. They were mostly on birds, but not all of them. One was about "The Coypu in Suffolk", and another on frogs and toads. In addition, he included the Dove family, the many wild and domestic varieties, including racing (homing) tumblers, mutations, etc. I still have a memento given me for my assistance in making this film by the boss man of Weetabix, one of the largest pigeon fanciers in the country. His flights (lofts) were something to be seen. Doug asked me if I would assist him at weekends to find material for these films. How could I resist!

One Saturday morning I called round to see Doug. His wife answered the door telling me he was at the rear of the house filming something. On approaching, I could see the camera all set up pointing into the small moat. He was filming a single batch of frogspawn. I said to him if he had the time I would take him to a prolific spawning spot. The next thing we were off in his Mark II Jaguar heading for the river that runs through Gt. Finborough Park near Stowmarket. There we found something very unusual, which I had never witnessed before in all my days. Frogs were mating with toads and toads mating with frogs. There were masses of frogspawn, which I am sure readers can visualise. The spawn of toads is completely different, long strings adhering to vegetation like pearl necklaces. Here they were not showing up well for filming. The next morning, Sunday, I took him to a lake at Drinkstone. It was a lovely calm sunny morning. There in the crystal clear shallows toads were spawning (no frogs). Their strings of spawn clung to the shoots of light green vegetation. Doug said it was wonderful and absolutely ideal for filming, He then asked me how I knew they were there. I replied that I knew every lake, pond and river in the area through my birding travels – I never missed much. We took samples of spawn from the Finborough mixed-mating back to headquarters and placed them in the time-lapse studio where cameras took photographs every two minutes to record there progress during hatching. I never did know what the outcome was of the mixed-mated spawn. Did they become togs or froads?

I did appear in a couple of films, feeling quite self-conscious in front of the cameras. If the film sequences were not completed in one weekend it was finalised the next but I had to wear exactly the same clothing, which was understandable.

Having my first insight into filmmaking seemed, in some cases, that what you start with and what you finish with can be completely different. During my very interesting time with

Doug he asked me one day why, with all my knowledge of birds and their behaviour, I had never thought of taking photographs of them, especially from a hide. He then went on to advise me on the type of camera and lenses that I would require for this purpose. After giving the idea some thought I decided this is what I would do. Eventually Doug and his family moved away to Mistley in Essex, also taking their dog Cleo.

Once, when Doug and his family were on location filming in the Faroes, I looked after Cleo. One evening, when taking her for a walk, she spied a cat. Her instincts right away were 'must chase' but puss held her ground, she would not be chased. On went Cleo's brakes and, with a little yelp of panic, received a pat round the face from the offended cat. It was like watching a cartoon.

I lost touch with Doug but after several years he returned, hoping I could help him with his filming. He wanted some footage of a large Starling roost, which he needed for Yorkshire TV. I knew where the roost was, and he got what he wanted. I never saw him again after that. I will always remember the enjoyment I derived from the whole experience.

I went into my bird photography in leaps and bounds. Firstly, I bought a Praktica SLR (single lens reflex) camera, a 135mm telephoto lens, mainly for hide work, and later, when I could afford it, a 400mm lens plus a 2-times converter and a light meter. That was all I needed, no such thing as digital in those days. All photographs were on slides at very low speeds.

As time passed, it became known that I had a collection of slides on birds. A Mrs. Williams came to see me. She lived with her husband in the mansion at Haughley Park. She asked me if I would give a talk illustrated with slides to the Wetherden Community Society. I declined saying I was far too shy to talk to an audience. In the end she persuaded me. On the night arranged, off I nervously went with projector, screen and slides in the hope that nothing would go wrong. Fifteen minutes into the talk we all went into darkness; I was panic-stricken. I heard Mr. Williams apologising for the interruption and saying that normal service would be resumed as soon as another 50p was put in the meter. What a relief that was. That first engagement broke the ice for me. I eventually overcame my shyness to give hundreds of talks to thousands of people, entertaining them with many anecdotes pertaining to my bird slides.

One Off Stories

Seek and Hide

They say "a bird in the hand is worth two in the bush" but to me the next best thing is sitting in a hide just a few feet away, seeing birds tending their young. Encouraged by my television friend, Doug Fisher, to take up bird photography, I have never looked back, only forward through a camera lens from within a hide.

A hide was the one essential piece of equipment I had yet to acquire. Working for the Stowmarket UDC during the 1960s, apart from workshop, mortuary, etc., there was at their depot what we called a paper shed. This was where the refuse vehicle brought waste cardboard and paper from around the town to be recycled. It was only by chance that I spied a large strong cardboard box about three feet square by four feet high. Believe it or not, this box was to become the first of many hides.

I set to work making the necessary aperture to receive the camera lens, and also slots in the sides for observing the surroundings wherever it was used. My next operation was to find a nest, preferably with young, to photograph. There is an important procedure in hide work. Once having found the chosen nest, the hide is placed some distance away moving it closer to the nest at intervals, possibly hours, making sure each time the birds accept this alien object in their territory. Some birds will adapt to the circumstances more readily than others. At no time must you risk the possibility of birds deserting. Remember you are the intruder in their space; patience is a virtue.

My first nest to start my photography was that of a Reed Bunting with young. Once my hide was in its final position, about six feet from the nest, I knocked down all the dead parsley stalks that they use as perches when working their way back to their nest. I then placed my own parsley stalk close to their nest. The only place that they could perch was on this stalk. I have used this method with other birds: Kingfishers, Grey Wagtails, etc., in later years. The Reed Buntings were very obliging, resulting in some nice photographs. However, there was another drawback, apart from the lack of height in my hide, I attracted the attention of a horse. This horse at times became very inquisitive, nudging the hide with its nose, I suppose wondering where I had gone, or what I was doing, not at all helpful. During its lifetime the horse had pulled a fruit and vegetable cart around the town until there was a collision with a vehicle, then sadly he had to be put to sleep.

My next move was in the same vicinity, to a Yellow Bunting's nest, which contained small young. It was about two feet off the ground in scrub. Unfortunately, this nest was not successful. Before my hide was anywhere near the nest the young died owing to a night of violent storms. My hide also suffered from the weather and I could see its days were numbered. When it eventually dried out I put it among mixed reeds and willow herb where there was much chattering of birds.

On my next visit I watched this area from a distance through binoculars. There was a pair of Red Warblers busy carrying nesting materials. I could hardly believe it when I found this nest, which was being built eighteen inches from my hide. Normally you put hide to nest, on this occasion it was nest to hide.

They completed their nest, laying the usual four eggs. During my absence a Cuckoo had visited, laying her egg and removing one of the Reed Warblers in that order. How fortunate it would have been had I been in my hide at the time she came; I could have photographed her every move, although over and done with in moments. Cuckoos lay their eggs every other day in the afternoons as opposed to every day in the morning as do the smaller birds. The sum total of hours I spent in my hide at this Reed Warbler's nest, up to the time the young Cuckoo fledged, was twenty-two. My cardboard box hide was now at the end of its life, I am surprised it lasted as long as it did.

* * *

My next hide was already on the drawing board. As luck would have it I acquired a quantity of waterproofed hessian from the same source as my previous hide (box). I made this hide two feet six by two feet six by five feet high. In this one I would be able to stretch my legs, whereas, when emerging after a couple of hours from the box, I walked about like Quasimodo. Fifty plus square feet of material was used, with sufficient left over for a second one (read on), and four 1" by 1" corner supports plus four guy ropes to tension the hide when erected. Birds become wary with material flapping in the wind.

I was now ready again to embark on my next nest. This time a Sedge Warbler's that I had previously found when it contained eggs. Now having small young, I was keen to get set up. Sedge Warblers normally build their nests very close to the ground, in sedge as its name suggests. This particular nest was an exception, being three feet from the ground. I have never seen one before or since at this height, very convenient for photography. Pleased with my first stint, I intended to return the following day, which I did only to find my new hide had been stolen. I left it on its site overnight not thinking it would come to harm, in fact, not thinking. I presumed it was children from the nearby housing estate. Luckily I managed to get some nice pictures of the Sedge Warbler and its cousin the Reed, both were very obliging subjects.

I decided that in the future no hide would be left unattended at any time. I made an identical hide from the material I had left over from the last one, which served me very well for many years as I pursued my nest photography.

***

I was working at my workbench one day when the foreman came to me saying, 'There are two CID officers who would like to have a word with you'. The two smartly dressed gentlemen asked me if I was Robert Copping and described the make, colour and registration of my car.

'Yes', I replied.

They went on to say they were investigating the appearance of my car on a number of occasions at various airfields: Wattisham, Rattlesden, Honington etc. and could I explain why this was so?

'Of course I can', I replied.

I told them that I was an ornithologist and that the large expanses attracted a number of migratory birds: large flocks of Golden Plovers a sprinkling of Wheatears, also Redstarts and Stonechats that liked to perch on the perimeter fences. After chatting for some while they seemed quite satisfied with my explanation. I heard nothing more.

***

Apart from the Plovers, the other birds mentioned would appear regularly every spring on the school playing field, where I lived.

During the 1960s I led the Stowmarket Naturalists Society on an annual I-spy bird outing at Claydon Quarries near Ipswich, at present the proposed site for the Snoasis project and an excellent place to see a wide variety of birds, i.e. breeding Yellow Wagtails, Red Shank, Wheatear, Shell Duck, etc. One pair of birds I saw I thought at first were Ringed Plovers but watching further revealed that they were a much rarer bird, namely the Little Ringed Plover. There are a few differences in plumage between these two birds; the main one I suppose is the lack of a white wing bar on the Little Ringed. These Plovers are summer visitors, arriving in March. They have a preference for sand and gravel pits in which to breed. They bred sporadically up to 1944. From then and after the war so many excavations for sand and gravel were worked for the national rebuilding programme (there were over 200 pits just around London) the Little Plovers took advantage of these sites to breed. These birds were next on my list to photograph.

The quarry manager knew I often visited, although I had no written permission to do so at the time. Officially these Plovers, their nests and eggs should not be photographed without a special licence from the necessary authorities, as they were quite scarce. Of course, I took notice of this! The eggs would have probably hatched by the time I obtained this licence. The nest was situated in the middle of a large flat plateau at the base of the quarry. As with other birds nesting in this situation (Plovers, Terns, Oystercatchers), they are easy to find when they are incubating their eggs. All you need to do is to sit at a distance and the birds will show where their nest is, otherwise you needn't bother. There is no particular nest, just a depression in the ground, the birds occasionally adding more stones or shells if available, more for decoration perhaps. The first thing I had to do was to adapt my hide so I could lift it a few inches and walk a few yards. It was going to be a long exercise. This was not too much of a problem. The main concern was that the hide would stand out like a sore thumb to the birds, and humans.

All kitted out with small collapsible seat, tripod, camera with a 400mm telephoto lens attached (can't remember food or drink) I started my long haul. The incubating bird was on/off her eggs each time I moved closer until my final move. I was about thirty yards from the nest. She became very suspicious, making a complete circuit of the hide, and this I thought was as far as I should go. I would have liked to be another ten yards closer. I was quite pleased with the photographs and it was worth all the effort involved.

Nest and eggs of the Little Ringed Plover

The following year I found another nest, this time at a working pit in the Gipping Valley, the Little Plovers showing no regard for the large bulldozer passing their nest only a few yards away.

Senseless Vandalism

A few years later I went to see Mr. & Mrs. Williams at their home in Haughley Park, asking if they would allow me to survey the bird life on their estate. They welcomed this idea. First I set about making a waterhole 4 feet by 3 feet and a little over 1 foot deep in the wooded area among bracken and silver birch trees, knowing that during a dry spell it would attract birds to drink and bathe. I find water a must for observing birds and this was as good a place as any to erect a hide for photography. With my past experience of EWS (emergency water supply), what we call waterholes in the Breckland conifer woods owned by Forest Enterprise, I found this very rewarding. After digging the hole I lined it with strong green mineral felt to make it appear natural and then filled it with water, which I transported in 5-gallon drums at least a quarter of mile from my car. I left it for several days for the birds to get accustomed to it. The day came when I put my hide, camera equipment, etc. in my car and was off with great expectations. When I arrived at the waterhole, which I had really worked hard on, I found it empty. Some vandal had taken a fork and riddled it with holes. It was not the work of children I am sure, as it was quite a distance from any houses. I never did find the culprit. The idea was then abandoned. Who would want to do such a senseless thing?

Caretaker/Teacher

I will now continue with events that occurred before the toilet-hide story.

It came about that in the early 1970s the Stowmarket Urban District Council was to amalgamate with the Mid Suffolk District Council. Prior to this being finalised, I was asked by my boss if I would be prepared to work at the latter Council's depot at Needham Market four miles away (this was not compulsory). The Stowmarket UDC tradesmen were going through a period involving time-and-motion studies and Council officers came with us daily recording every minute of our work. Time sheets were the next thing for us. Working at Needham Market would mean travelling back and forth daily, having to start again with packed lunches, not to mention leaving my workmates and all my town friends. Giving the proposal much thought, I decided that this was not for me. The second carpenter was also asked; he likewise refused, and the third was not asked, as he had no transport.

During this unsettling period an advert appeared in the Press asking for a caretaker at Combs Middle School, just out of town. This school had been built for two years and had a new bungalow now ready for the elected caretaker to live in on site.

The existing caretaker had his own property in the town and was not prepared to give that up. I was quite happy to move from the building trade so I applied for the job. On the day of the interviews I received a letter from my old building firm, O. Seaman & Son, asking me to return, enticing me with well over the rate of pay. I ignored this. I don't know how they got wind of my intention. When the interviews had been completed, it was whittled down to two of us. Several times we went back and forth into the interview room but in the end I got the job. I think the fact that I was a carpenter played a big part in their decision. I assume the headmaster was thinking ahead, as he knew that the retirement of their woodwork teacher was imminent. Later I was approached and asked if I would fill this position. After interviews with the school governors and higher officials, I was given the job. I now had two jobs at the school.

We moved into the bungalow, which had quite a nice-sized front and rear garden. The lounge faced south overlooking the school's playing field, and the large Combs Wood now managed by the Suffolk Wildlife Trust. Looking north was wild open country, and the proposed site for a new private housing estate.

The rear garden could not be worked for a while owing to a pair of Skylarks that had taken up residence with their young. I thought, 'How convenient was that!'. The large open grassland that we overlooked also had a few pairs of Skylarks plus another interesting little bird, the Grasshopper Warbler, recognised by its strange song. Its incessant reeling song, like an electric sewing machine seemingly without a break, gives away its position. I never found this nest, as they are difficult to locate, unseen from above and very close to, or on, the ground. I have only found one, which was in Northfield Wood at Onehouse near Stowmarket. There were a few isolated trees and hedgerows on this open grassland that were home to numerous birds: Linnets and Common and Lesser Whitethroats.

Bullfinch nest with six eggs

I also found a Bullfinch's nest in the brambles with a rare set of six eggs, the only six I have ever found; they were as beautiful as the bird's plumage.

My move to the school was beneficial in more ways than one.

A Loo with a View

Hide work is normally a straightforward procedure. With the previous stories they were different or amusing, but before I embark on another aspect of my life with birds, I have one more story, which my audiences find quite funny.

Several years ago I had friends whose two sons were into motocross (scrambling). Sundays would take them to events far and wide, their van loaded with their bikes and other paraphernalia that went with the sport, including a portable toilet. This toilet was a tubular structure, tarpaulin-covered (green) with zip fastening about two foot six inches square by five feet high. Through the years they ventured from scrambling into speedway, so the toilet was no longer needed and was stored in their shed. I became the next owner of this toilet, ideal for my photographic purposes, hence the title of this story. It was the best hide I ever had, and still use to this day.

I was to photograph a Common White Throat, a summer-visiting Warbler that had small young. I had worked through the morning hours on this loo-cum-hide and it was now in a position that the birds accepted. It is an advantage if someone accompanies me to the hide, leaving me inside and then walking away. The birds will carry on feeding almost right away. If I am alone I suppose they wonder what is going on and will take longer to resume feeding. Unfortunately on this occasion I was alone, but luckily there was a footpath fifty yards away. Within fifteen minutes a young couple aged about 20 years old came walking along. I said to the young fellow 'Excuse me, would you kindly accompany me to my hide', He looked at me in a curious manner (wouldn't anyone, there are some strange people about these days). I explained to him the reason for this request and he was happy to oblige. Before we went into the hide he asked if he could see the nest. I think he was still a bit dubious. Upon looking around the hide he actually saw the bird shielding the young from the sun. I thanked him for his time and off he went. The birds continued to feed within minutes. After taking the photographs I tried to conceal the nest roughly in the same way I found it. Not much could be done to the small area where I had been sitting about six feet from the nest.

Common Whitethroat feeding chicks

* * *

I mentioned earlier that some birds more than others will accept a hide encroaching on its nest. I have read at some stage that Blackcaps, on seeing a hide, will remove their young into the surrounding vegetation. I once found a Blackcap's nest with young among nettles. There was no other place to erect my hide but six feet away. The two birds accepted this closeness. At times the little chocolate-brown-capped female would brood the young until the male came to feed. With its cousin, the Garden Warbler, I had an identical situation, only this time the nest was in brambles. After placing my hide close to this nest (again with small young) I retreated to a distance watching for their acceptance. Nothing seemed untoward. When I did settle in my hide there was only one young left. She had removed the other three somewhere into the brambles. I only took one photograph of her feeding the single chick and then I departed. They could obviously see danger approaching. The small young had hardly any feathers. Did she/they bring the young back to this nest after I went? I returned two/three weeks later and took the empty nest for my collection. From the amount of feather scale in the nest I would say that they did return the rest of their young once the danger had passed.

Apart from their appearance, these two summer-visiting Warblers are alike in many ways. Their song, habitat, nest and eggs are similar. One has to see the birds at their nest to be really sure.

Wigwam

A naturalist friend of mine, who worked as a storeman for George Thurlow the agricultural engineering firm at Stowmarket, asked me if I would like a piece of green tarpaulin which had become surplus to requirements. I went to visit him right away and after seeing this tarpaulin I estimated that it would be large enough for another hide. I transported the material to my workshop until such time as I could make the new hide. This one was to be three-sided, making it easier to erect and having no need for guy ropes. The tarpaulin had brass eyelets that I could fasten when I was inside.

Using creosote, I painted small trees on the three sides to break up the outline. Once erected it was like a wigwam. To give it a trial I took it to Tostock Low Meadows, erected it in a gangway at the bottom of a field near the rush-bordered small river, in the hope of seeing the secretive Water Rail. I had heard and seen this bird in this location at various times. On my left was a large hawthorn hedge going back to the Norton road and I had taken along a few apples hoping to attract them, or any other wildlife. Water Rails will eat almost anything, be it animal or vegetable, but apples do feature in their diet. It was a lovely calm sunny afternoon. I settled down and waited for signs of movement that was soon to come but in another form. Within half-an-hour the peacefulness was broken by the sound of gunshots coming from my left and getting closer all the time. I became aware that the farmers were having a shoot, that's all I needed! Keeping a watchful eye through the slots in my hide, I first saw two black retriever dogs appear through a clearing near the road, followed by half a dozen men with guns. They stopped in their tracks upon seeing my wigwam-style hide. After a lengthy discussion one gent with gun approached my hide putting his fingers through one of the slots. In a gruff voice he said 'Is there anyone in there?' 'Yes',

I replied and explained what my mission was about. 'Don't you think you should have asked permission before coming here', he said. I told him that as three different farmers owned the meadows I didn't know which belonged to whom. At no time did I show myself. Soon after our encounter I packed up and made for home.

One evening a couple of weeks later I was back again to have a general look round. I spotted a chap in the distance coming in my direction, if I hadn't wanted him to see me I would have remained still. (Movement draws attention.) I carried on towards him until we met. We chatted for several minutes and I told him that I was a regular visitor to their meadows going back to my childhood days. During our conversation he asked if I was the chap who was in 'that wigwam thing' a couple of weeks ago. I replied that I was, which brought a smile to his face. 'It certainly got us thinking at the time', he said. Before we went our separate ways he told me that I could visit anytime I wanted, for which I thanked him. I never did get my Water Rail photographs from there. Like many people I obtained them from Lackford Lakes near Bury St. Edmunds where the birds regularly feed during the winter months under the feeders outside the visitors' centre.

Cemetery Flycatchers

During my illustrated talks to clubs and societies I mention odd stories, which some find amusing, this is one such story.

The setting was in a cemetery in Stowmarket where I planned to photograph Spotted Flycatchers. I was working for the Stowmarket UDC (Urban District Council) at the time, which gave me right of way. Spotted Flycatchers arrive here from Africa for the summer, normally rearing one brood, on occasions two. For these little birds cemeteries are a favoured site, as well as for many others, especially the Goldcrest, our smallest bird. The environment is peaceful with no interference from the residents. As their name suggests, they feed entirely on flies, butterflies, etc. catching them from a chosen perch, perhaps a low branch where they return each time. The female also eats small snails and woodlice to give her the calcium she needs to form her eggshells. The chosen perch for the one I wished to photograph was a headstone to a grave. I set my hide on top of this grave, which had a marble surround with granite chippings. All was nice and quiet and I was taking some good photographs when I heard boys' voices coming from the nearby road. I could see the two boys through my observation side slots. They became quieter when they noticed my hide.

Their curiosity got the better of them and they decided to investigate what my hide was and what it was doing there. Unknown to them I was inside. Coming through a gap in the hawthorn hedge, they gingerly approached the hide. When they got within a couple of yards I let out a terrible moan. With that they went like bolts from a crossbow straight through a gap in the hedge and up the road, not to return. I sat chuckling to myself.

Spotted Flycatcher

***

I would have liked to have found the nest of another pair of Spotted Flycatchers, this time at Onehouse just outside Stowmarket. Given time I'm sure I would have been successful. One of the pair was a leucistic form. I will enlighten those who are not familiar with the word 'leucistic': an albino bird is white with pink eyes and a melanistic is black, often seen in pheasants. A leucistic form is white with all soft parts, eyes, beak and legs a natural colour making them very attractive birds. I have a reasonable slide of this bird.

Stowmarket Naturalist's Society

Going back over fifty years to when I joined the Stowmarket Naturalists Society, meetings were held monthly on a Monday. The first meeting I attended I sat on my own not knowing a soul.

It was an added interest for members to bring along exhibits to chat about. The second meeting I attended I took along a dead male Scoter (not scooter). I found this bird, one of the sea ducks, washed up on the beach the day before at Sizewell. The forty plus members showed much interest.

There were only two other members who were interested in birds. They normally sat together, so I joined them at future meetings. The younger of the two spent most of his leisure time on the coast at Walberswick, where he and others manned a Heligoland bird trap. All data on each bird trapped was monitored and, after a ring was attached, released back into the wild. A very interesting and worthwhile project.

I was invited to spend the odd weekend with him but declined the offer thinking it was unfair to my wife and son. They always looked forward to our birding weekends together, whether inland or coastal.

Our friendship came to an untimely end when he was killed by a vehicle while cycling from his home at Needham Market to his workplace at Stowmarket.

The second gentleman was elderly, a bank manager soon to retire. I will refer to him as JR.

My Introduction to Breckland

JR was an authority on birds of the Breckland. We soon became very close friends, spending many hours/days through the years in this unique, diverse area. It's hard to visualise what the Breckland was like hundreds of years ago, enormous areas of heath, warrens and meres. These meres, mostly natural with the odd one man-made, fluctuate yearly in water levels, from brimming full to completely dry. When they do hold water there is a greater variety of wildlife (Ducks, Grebes) than anywhere else in the country.

In 1922 the Breck landscape changed dramatically when the Forestry Commission planted vast areas of conifer trees, which themselves are quite quiet during the birds' breeding season. It's the area where the Forestry Commission fell and replant that becomes ideal habitats for a number of species. As rich as this area is for natural history, one can roam about and see precious little. It's knowing what to look for and where to find it that's important.

One creature you cannot possibly fail to see is the rabbit, introduced in bygone years from Europe. The sandy soil suited them so they became extremely numerous, resulting in their being caught in their millions in various ways for their flesh and fur.

Prior to the outbreak of myxomatosis in the 1950s, it was estimated there were forty million rabbits in the country, the Breck being the most populated area. During this time the disease nearly wiped out the entire rabbit population. Today their numbers could well be back to the pre-myxomatosis days. To read in detail about the farming of the rabbits and other aspects of the Breck there is an excellent book called "The

Background to Breckland" written by H.J. Mason and A. McClelland.

Through the years I spent a lot of time in this wonderful Breckland area with my family and JR.

I acquired a permit from the Forestry Commission allowing me access to all of the forests, and was also fortunate to have a permit for all the Elveden Estates owned by Lord Iveagh.
I held this permit for twelve years before I let it lapse. I obtained my permit with the help of my filming friend, Doug Fisher, who in turn knew Philip Wayre, another filming friend of Anglia TV, who was a custodian for the Elveden Estates at that time.

It's not so much what you know but who you know!

Man with a Gun

Travelling around the Breckland during the winter months can be quite rewarding, one never knows what delights will make your day. On one occasion my family and I came across an amazing sight at Eriswell. A huge flock of Greenfinches, numbering many thousands, was feeding on arable land when allowed to do so as they were frequently preyed upon by a male Hen Harrier, in itself a lovely bird to see.

Large numbers of Bramblings were seen at Kilverstone, under beech trees, feeding on the mast. This particular year was, as we call it, a Brambling year; other years they could be absent. We would alternate our weekend outings going to either the Breck or the coast. This account was from the coast.

We travelled to Dunwich Forest and, would you believe it, we came across exactly the same thing as we had at Eriswell, with the Greenfinch and the Hen Harrier. I was told that a ringing project was taking place at their roost.

Slaughden (Aldburgh) was another favourite place up near the Martello tower, where one could often see Snow Buntings and Shore Larks. There, one afternoon, we saw approximately 400 White Fronted Geese flying in from the sea to go down to graze in fields, out of sight, at Sudbourne. We set out to find these geese.

We found them feeding in fields some distance from a solitary farmhouse. I stopped here hoping to get permission to go and photograph the birds. As I couldn't locate anyone I just carried on, stopping at a five-barred gate. I got out of the car and was climbing over the gate when I heard someone say, 'Where do you think you're off to?' There was a man with a shotgun. I told him what I wanted to do and that I had called at the house to ask permission. He then said I was not to go into the field. I told him that it would do no harm to take a couple of pictures, but he was adamant. I climbed over the gate and took my photos, when I returned he had gone. I didn't think for a moment that he would shoot me, although I did expect him to fire the gun to put the birds into flight, just to be awkward.

Often as not we would finish our day calling at the strand overlooking the river Orwell. If the sun was out it was a bonus having the light behind us to view the many birds: large numbers of Waders, several species of Duck, if lucky Slavonian Grebes and Red Breasted Mergansers.

I have always highly rated the Orwell during the winter months.

Stowmarket Naturalist's Society Outing

It was now the month of May, time for me to lead the Stowmarket Naturalist Society on their annual bird outing. The destination I chose was West Stow, near Icklingham, before it became a Country Park.

After leaving our cars, carrying binoculars and cameras, the first bird we sighted was an Osprey hovering beyond the river Lark in search of fish in one of the lakes in Lackford. This complex of lakes, now belong to the Suffolk Wildlife Trust.

After an enjoyable walk round the eighteen-acre lake, during which we saw a number of Ducks and Grebes, etc., I took the party across the road from the main entrance into the fir forest where there was a recently established heronry.

Herons are our second earliest nesting birds. Heronries are found mostly in the vicinity of lakes and tidal rivers where there is a good food source: eels, frogs, fish and other aquatic life. I have never seen a heronry in conifer trees, but it could have been overlooked in its early days, since it would be difficult to see in this type of habitat.

We walked under their nests where the remnants could be seen of discarded blue/green eggshells from the hatchings. I spied a young Heron on the ground, probably over enthusiastic to leave its nest. The young are in the nest anything up to two months before they fly. I made haste and caught this youngster, making sure not to have my eyes taken out with its long pointed beak. Mind you, I was younger and fitter then; it would have given me a run for my money nowadays. After the members had satisfied their curiosity, I released the bird.

An eventful afternoon was had by all. Starting and finishing with two birds was a bonus in itself; quite unexpected

Another heronry I frequently visited was on the fringe of Breckland. This was on the Ampton Estate approximately four miles north of Bury St, Edmunds. This heronry was an old established one situated in larch trees close to a very large lake (third largest in Suffolk). After a couple of visits I thought I would write to the estate office, requesting permission to enter the heronry, in order to survey the lake for wildfowl. In fact I wrote twice, enclosing a stamped addressed envelope each time. No reply came, so as they didn't say I couldn't go, I just went.   There was a house opposite the wood that I called at, asking if they would allow me to park my car outside their property while I went into the wood. They kindly agreed that this would be OK. If a gamekeeper passed by he would take it for granted that they had visitors. One day I took a friend with me who was interested in seeing the heronry. Picking him up at Tostock on my way. We were walking down the woodland track when we met a party of six people, all wearing their green attire, my friend wanted to turn back, I said, 'Just carry on walking', when they passed I said, 'Good morning, lovely day', they replied in agreement assuming we had right of way! When all was clear we climbed to one nest, which held two eggs, this was on February 4th. The only drawback on my visits was that all the Herons would go and stand in front of the big Hall, like a platoon of soldiers. Anyone seeing them would know someone was at the heronry.   At no time was I approached.

Inquisitive Forest Rangers

Every year the committee members of the Stowmarket Naturalist Society would meet to discuss who would be asked to come and give us a talk on whatever topic. I was put down for one on a yearly basis. I think they took me for granted, although I never tire of seeing my own slides.

One member would insist that all slides shown were new to them. It's not easy to produce sixty–seventy fresh slides every year considering I only had weekends and perhaps the odd summer evening to take photographs. To supplement my talk I had a collection of nests of some smaller British birds. These were kept in two cardboard flower boxes partitioned off for individual nests, about thirty in all. A notice was put with them explaining that all nests were taken after the birds had no further use for them, either when deserted or the young had flown.

Once a year we held an 'open night' (I was the main attraction of the show) held in the lecture theatre at the Stowmarket Grammar School, now the Stowmarket High. It was well advertised for all and sundry to attend, perhaps gaining a few members to our already good membership at the same time, which was approximately 50. There was no entry fee to the 'open night' but if anyone wished to place money in a pot on leaving to show their appreciation they could do so.

After the meeting had finished there was usually someone wanting to chat. On this occasion everyone had gone, apart from two gentlemen. I asked them what I could do for them. Apparently they, like everyone else, had shown interest in the nest exhibits, noticing that there were three nests of Red-backed Shrikes, each nest slightly different in their construction. They asked me where I obtained them. I replied

'Sorry, I am not going to tell you. I don't know who you are'. Whereupon they produced identification showing that they were forest rangers, working for Forest Enterprise. 'I am still not telling you. To me your identification could just be a cover'. With that they said, 'We will tell you where you got them. The first nest was from a dog rose bush in the overgrown sandpit at Santon Downham, the second a couple of hundred yards further down the road in a hawthorn bush and the third was near the car park but didn't contain young'. They were right on all counts, although the third nest did have young because I took a photograph of them when they were small, after which they were probably taken by a cage-bird fanatic for their aviary. The rangers could see that there was no feather scale in the nest, which would be normal if the young had successfully fledged.

Their next question was, 'Why did I take them?' I explained that egg collectors travelled around likely haunts during the winter months when there is no foliage on the bushes. They know a Red-backed Shrikes nest and would return the following year in the first week in June for their eggs, knowing they will be in that vicinity. They accepted my explanation, thanked me for an interesting evening, and left.

* * *

Red-backed Shrike eggs are sought after because they are beautiful and with many variations. If lucky enough one may well come across an erythritic-type (red variety).

I have met eggers, as we call them, at Bucklesham, near Ipswich, coming all the way from Scotland for their eggs.

* * *

One nest I was pleased to have in my collection was of the Hawfinch (our largest finch). These birds are seldom seen during the breeding season owing to their very secretive nature. I obtained this nest at West Stow near Icklingham. I am sure I see nests of this species during my travels, which resemble small Rooks' nests.

There is one other little bird that is another of my favourites, the Lesser Redpoll. They build the smallest nest in the country, although not the smallest bird. The actual cup of the nest is a mere 1½" across. It is also one of the most substantially built and will hold together through extreme weather where other birds' nests will disintegrate.

* * *

There is a law stating that it is illegal to take birds' nests before October. By this time the nests are just not worth having. If one knows what he is doing I cannot see a problem.

Injured Kestrel

A friend, who had been out during the evening shooting pigeons, knocked at my door one evening holding a box. Inside this box was an injured male Kestrel. As the light was fast fading he shot what he thought was a low-flying Pigeon coming over a hedge only to find it was a Kestrel. It was not seriously injured, but was unable to fly. His first thought was me, as I used to treat sick and wounded birds. Over the years, I had many birds brought to me: Barn Owls, Golden Plover, Swift, etc. In fact I never knew what would arrive. Some, unfortunately, were beyond treatment. As much as I disliked killing anything, these were put to sleep humanely.

I took this Kestrel out of the box to examine. He didn't seem too distressed. Straight away he took hold of my thumb with his beak close to my nail. Blood started to flow, not to mention the pain that went with it. I put the bird back into the box after he decided to let go of my bleeding thumb. I went indoors, where by wife administered first aid (to me!). My next move wasn't a good one either. I was curious to find out how powerful his bite really was. Offering the bird my finger, which was fairly hardened through work, I discovered that was the worst thing I could have done. He took hold with his beak in a vice-like grip, causing a lot of pain but not breaking the skin. I very quickly put the bird back in the box.

My next move wasn't much better. I thought if I covered his head with a sort of hood like one does in falconry, he would remain quiet when being handled. This I did with my young daughter's sock. On picking up the bird (sock on head) for the third time, he somehow managed to get one of its talons underneath one of my fingernails; more pain and a lot more blood, much more blood. With plasters on my finger and thumb, I did get to examine his wing and found nothing too serious. As the bird seemed all right I put him in a cage in my greenhouse.

Hoping I didn't have to force-feed him, I gingerly offered him his first meal: a small dead bird found on the road. He took it from my fingers, plucked and ate it. That was a relief. From then on it was a matter of feeding him a varied diet: small birds, mice, worms, even beef mince.

As the weeks went by, we became quite friendly but I didn't attempt to handle him. He was a lovely bird, as were all the birds of prey. One day it all went wrong, I accidentally left the greenhouse door ajar. He was out of his cage, also the greenhouse, like a flash, then across a small area of ploughed land. I tried to catch him but his flight was much improved although he couldn't gain height, eventually going
under a 6'chain-link fence into a hawthorn-covered dry ditch which bordered a large forest. I had lost him.

I worried about him being vulnerable to predators, as he couldn't fly. The next time I saw him a couple of days later, he was perched on an angle-iron stay of the chainlink fence at the corner of the wood. Then to my surprise and delight, I saw something wonderful. A female kestrel came with a morsel and fed him. What a lovely thing to happen. From then on I knew he was to make a full recovery and possibly a mate as well?

Kestrel

79

Kestrel nest

Five baby Kestrels, one sleeping.

The Swift

I mentioned the Swift as one of the many bird casualties brought to me. This arrived one afternoon in the saddlebag of a friend's cycle. My first thought was how on earth could I keep and feed this bird, as its diet is entirely of insects that they catch on the wing. Its whole life, with the exception of the breeding season is spent in the air. Swifts come here from Africa just for the summer, arriving about the 1st of May departing during August, sometimes only rearing one young, which it feeds for six weeks. They are not related to the Martins or Swallows.

This was now late July. I first did a quick inspection, which showed no apparent sign of injury. I pitched it into the air hoping that it would become airborne. Back to the ground it came. Swifts rarely come to ground, as they cannot take off owing to their very short legs and long wings.

More thorough examination revealed three primary (flight) feathers were damaged, probably from hitting wires in their colonial gathered flights at this time of the year. After much thought, I got my nail clippers and carefully cut these three feathers off just beyond the damaged area. I then proceeded to cut three good feathers from the opposite wing the exact length of the other, balancing the two wings. I again offered it into the air. This time it took to the skies. It made two circuits around my property, finally flying very low over me as if to say thank you. How satisfied I felt to think it could now fly back to Africa in the coming weeks.

Little Grebe

The photograph of the Little Grebe shown was one I rescued.

I received a telephone call one morning from a Mr. R.J.
Copping (my namesake, only his Christian name was Rodney).
At the time, he was the manager of Combs Tannery just
outside Stowmarket. He, like many others, knew I dealt with
sick and wounded birds.

The adult Little Grebe

He informed me of a bird that he thought was in distress and
would I go to investigate.

'What species of bird is it?' I asked. 'A Cormorant', came the
reply. I wondered how I was going to keep it, as it eats a few
pounds of fish everyday.

When I arrived at the Tannery there was a gathering of onlookers peering into a concrete enclosure that was about 12 feet square and 5 feet deep containing a couple of feet of stagnant water. I looked inside, expecting to see a large black bird but it turned out to be a Little Grebe, the smallest member of the Grebe family (relief!). I eventually caught this little bird, which wasn't an easy task I can assure you.

I took it home and checked it out; it didn't seem distressed at any time. Before releasing the bird I took a few photographs

This little bird wasn't really using its brain when it descended into the tank of water. If not for me it would have been imprisoned, possibly for the rest of its life, which could have been short. As with all diving birds, Little Grebe have to run quite a distance before taking flight; this had nowhere to run. I released it on the school playing field. It was lovely to see this little bird frantically working its feet and wings before taking flight. Mind you, a Cormorant would have been in the same predicament.

Waterholes (E.W.S.)

Anyone who wished to see Crossbill, Siskin, Brambling and numerous other birds, even Red Squirrel and Grass Snakes, I would direct them to my favourite waterhole named 'Mayday' after the farm/smallholding on the opposite side of the road running between Elveden and Brandon.

The Forestry Commission had these waterholes (E.W.S. Emergency Water Supply) scattered around the forest that were filled by rainwater. My wife and son would sit in the nearby car making me aware of birds that were about to come down.

My hide at 'Mayday' emergency water supply.

There were also two excellent waterholes down the Icknield Way, a track that runs through the Kings Forest between North and West Stow, Icklingham. In later years all these waterholes were filled in, probably owing to heath and safety. I was given grid reference numbers to a few remaining ones in the forest. Although a little dilapidated, they still attracted wild life. I had special permission to take my car into the forest to transport my hide and equipment, as it was unsafe to leave it at the ride entrances where it was prone to vandalism.

I was provided with a key to all padlocks and, at the same time, I had keys for the forests at Rendlesham, Tunstall through to Dunwich.

Red Letter Day in 1968

During October 1968 I heard that there were a number of very rare visitors from Siberia visiting part of the coast. They were Slender Billed Nutcrackers, members of the Crow family, about the size of a Jackdaw.

Although I'm not a twitcher, the following Sunday my family and I set off to where there were sightings near Shingle Street. After a fruitless drive round (it was a chance thing anyway) we stopped by the roadside in the shade of a large tree to have a bite to eat and drink. During this time, a piece of bark dropped on to the bonnet of the car. Looking up from the window, I saw a Nutcracker probing the dead bark looking for insects, grubs, etc. When at home in Siberia its main diet is seeds.

Nutcracker on pole

Photographing birds was fairly new to me at that time, although I did manage to obtain thirteen pictures that I thought were acceptable. The Nutcracker flew down from the above branch onto the road quite close to us, then back to the branch. Moments later it was back on the road again before it flew across to a telegraph pole, its flight was similar to a Jay's.

When I had the photographs (slides) processed, I couldn't wait to see my results. I projected them on to a screen only to notice something different about the birds; one had a ring on its leg, the other hadn't. I had unknowingly photographed two Nutcrackers at the time. I had assumed there was only one, as the two birds didn't appear together. How lucky was I! The previous record for these birds in Suffolk was a single bird on a very stormy night in 1922.

Thetford Warren

It was in 1832 that the Great Bustard last bred in the country, the final ones in Suffolk on the barren Brecklands bordering Thetford Warren. In 1900, fifteen pinioned birds were introduced and released in Suffolk from Spain with the hope of starting a breeding herd, to no avail. The disappearance of these majestic birds was thought to be from farming methods, like so many of our birds today.

Thetford Warren Lodge, with its thick flint walls, small windows downstairs and front entrance doorway, was built on high ground from where marauding gangs could be observed. The Lodge in its heyday was a rabbit factory, receiving anything up to a quarter of a million rabbits a year for skinning, their pelts stretched out on racks in the adjacent buildings. In 1935 a fire destroyed two wings of the Lodge and all the wooden buildings; only the central tower remained.

Thetford Warren Lodge

88

Thetford Warren, enclosed by forestry, is today a very small area compared with bygone days. The Lodge is now a monument and is enclosed by a wrought iron fence, including the entrance door, to prevent access. Bird-wise it is nothing to what it was thirty years ago. My family and I could sit in the car having a picnic and see many breeding birds: Tree Pipit, Woodlark, Yellow Wagtail, Wheatear and, on occasion, a Red-backed Shrike. One would be very fortunate to see any of these birds nowadays.

My wife and son Adrian were looking through into the building from the doorway when Adrian commented that he could see a nest in a hole. The hole was approximately four inches by four inches, and may have been used in the past for dropping things down onto unwanted intruders. I put my arm up to the nest, feeling for the eggs and, bringing one out, I identified it as a Common Redstart, a summer visitor that is seldom seen.

Nest of six Yellow Wagtail young

Often an ice cream van would stop on the roadside, which was always welcome (still is), and while waiting for a couple to be served, I watched a Yellow Wagtail feed its young in its nest in the bank-side beside the road. A lovely photograph was taken of the six almost fledged young. What happened to these glorious days?

In late March, J.R. and I would go birding in search of Woodcock in what we called the Thetford Lows, a short walk from the Warren. It is a damp area with deciduous trees bordering the River Little Ouse, an ideal habitat not just for Woodcock but for our three resident Woodpeckers and Willow Tits also. Woodcock are nocturnal birds that nest on the ground, very difficult to locate as its plumage blends so well with the surrounding leaf colourings. There is only one other bird more camouflaged and that is the summer visiting Nightjar. I will write about them later.

Finding the nests of Woodcock is not easy by any means. One has to lightly tap around trees and any likely spots with a stick until such time as you disturb one of the birds, most likely the male who would take flight first distracting you from its sitting mate, which is usually no more than twenty feet radius from where he flies. One nest we found by chance on the 28th March had the usual four eggs; unfortunately a predator had eaten them, only the shells remained.

They also nest in the fir forests among bracken but there is such a large area to cover it is tiring work looking for them and not very rewarding.

***

Woodcocks by roadside

One year, during a holiday with my family in the Lake District, we were driving along the road near Hawes Water when I saw two Woodcock sitting together in the sunlight at the base of a stone wall. I quickly stopped the car. On getting out, a third bird, unseen at first, took flight. The other two remained, enabling me to take a couple of nice photographs. For Woodcock to be seen in daylight is a rare occurrence.

Lakenheath Warren

Lakenheath Warren is an extensive area of coarse grass, heather and bracken; in years gone by it was much larger, before the MOD requisitioned land for the aerodrome. It's part of Lord Iveagh's estate and a permit is required before venturing on to it. It was a favourite haunt for my family and me. We would spend a couple of hours there, sitting in the car or on the grass just watching the varied wildlife.

Lakenheath Warren as it was forty years ago.

Driving down the grass track one Sunday, I saw a bird in flight in the distance. Stopping the car I got out, with binoculars, intending to identify this bird but was distracted by a Common Curlew, which flew from its nest some thirty feet away.
I very quietly walked towards the spot and found the nest, containing four eggs.

Common Curlew

Curlew's nest with eggs

There were only four pairs of curlew nesting on the Warren at that time. They were first found to be nesting there in 1948 by the Lowestoft Field Club. Their wonderful call during the breeding period is unfamiliar in Suffolk, bringing back memories of our holidays further north in Yorkshire and the Lake District. They are our largest wader, mostly seen during the winter months on our tidal rivers and having one brood a season, laying their eggs in the first week of May.

On my next visit, a week later, I drove down the same track stopping in the area of the Curlew's nest, only this time I didn't switch the engine off. Stealthily walking with camera, plus 400mm telephoto lens, the bird remained on her eggs for me to take some good photographs. She remained undisturbed. If I had switched the car engine off as before, she would have flown. Finding their nests is difficult in such a large area and watching them from the car can be quite a long job. She will walk past her nest a few times before she feels safe enough to return to her eggs.

Young Common Curlew

Another time a suspicious van appeared on the Warren stopping some distance from us. After about one and a half hours a person from the van came over to us to see who we were. I explained my presence and he did also. He told me his name, which was known to me, and that he was a bird photographer, which I also knew. Had he any other intentions? I didn't trust him. He lived at Lakenheath where there was another chap who was a prolific egg collector (I have been out with him). He knew more about the birds of the Breckland than anyone and is mentioned in many books.

Among the variety of nesting birds on the Warren there was one, an attractive little bird slightly smaller than a Sparrow and quite scarce, called the Whinchat, a cousin of the Stonechat. It comes here from its wintering quarters in tropical Africa, hopefully rearing two broods. There were only two or three pairs nesting on the warren. JR and I only knew of one other nesting site of two pairs. They nest close to, or on, the ground in a mixture of grass and bracken. I always found their nests easy to locate by sitting in my car watching the male bird escorting his mate back to the nest. Strangely, the eggs of both the Whinchat and the Stonechat are bluish and faintly spotted with red. I don't know of any other ground nesting bird with eggs of this colouring. Wheatears also lay blue eggs, but they are hidden out of sight in rabbit burrows and suchlike.

Nowadays I believe the Whinchat has ceased to breed in the Suffolk Breck, whereas the Stonechat has increased somewhat in number.

Beyond the boundary of Lakenheath Warren on the southern side, the terrain is completely different, with grass cropped short, (probably by rabbits), scattered gorse bushes and flint stones; this is ideal habitat for the Stone Curlew, a summer visitor mainly arriving in March, although the odd ones have been observed over the winter months. They are not related to the Common Curlew, their feet are different, having three toes, similar to the Bustards. In my early days they were reasonably plentiful throughout the Breckland, especially the Icklingham Plains area. As a ground-nesting bird they have many natural predators; one they can do without is man, who takes their eggs for personal gain. The RSPB have a band of watchers during the breeding season to help these birds to breed successfully. Their numbers are increasing slowly and are now around 80-90 pairs.

The Stone Curlew

One brood is normal, sometimes two. The two eggs are laid in a shallow scrape on the bare ground during the first week of May. The only other bird with eggs similar in shape and colouring is the Oystercatcher. I don't know whether it's by chance or deliberate that the eggs are laid head to tail to each other.

If they are successful in rearing young they will return the following year and lay their eggs in the exact scrape as the year before.

Stone Curlews nest with eggs

They become active in the evenings, making their strange wailing calls that one would not associate coming from a bird.

While outside at night I have heard their call echoing eerily over the countryside. When danger threatens they remain motionless, flattening their bodies close to the sandy ground. Let's hope their numbers continue to rise, as they are truly a Breckland bird.

Two young Stone Curlew

The Punt at Drinkstone

As the years progressed, I was still drawn to my childhood haunt, the Tostock Low Meadows. Often after my visits there I would sometimes make a detour on the way home, calling in at Drinkstone Lake a couple of miles from Tostock. Drinkstone Lake is approximately nine acres in extent set in an attractive park. Through the years it has become very silted. The largest open area can be seen from the road. It then continues through a very reedy middle part to another small open area at the far end. There is a boathouse with a flat-bottomed boat (punt) and a beanpole of about eight feet to manoeuvre the boat about. Incidentally, there is also an icehouse a couple of hundred yards from the lake, the only one I know of. I have never thought to check this for bats. I would say it is an ideal place for them.

On one of my visits there, I saw, resting near the reeds, a very attractive male Pochard Duck (one of the diving group). I found the female sitting on her nest, which was well hidden among the reeds just above water level. I wanted a photograph of this nest for my collection. The first thing I did was to write to Bury St. Edmunds to the Secretary of the Angling Club who had fishing rights for the lake. I requested permission to use the boat for about an hour. I received a letter from him explaining that the boat was at Bury St. Edmunds being repainted. I knew this to be untrue; the boat was still in the boathouse. A polite way to say I couldn't use the boat! After reading many of my stories I am sure you know what's coming next. The next fine calm evening I took a friend with me to the lake. After boarding the boat we punted to the reed bed where the nest was. Using the sturdy beanpole, we levered the square-ended boat into the reeds. After reaching the nest I photographed the eight eggs - that was the easy part. From then on unforeseen problems arose. I hope readers can visualise what I am trying to explain in this continuing story. This boat is flat-bottomed with lateral ribs across the hull. The reeds were last year's growth and, being brittle, they broke off in the same direction, as the boat was moving. However, coming back, the broken-off reeds were facing the wrong way and caught onto the ribs of the boat. This resulted in using extra force on the pole as progress was slow but it became much slower when the pole broke! The evening light was fast fading. We were fortunate that the water was not too deep in this area as we only had half a pole. By the time we eventually got out of the reeds it was totally dark. To get the boat back to the boathouse was nigh on impossible. The area of water to cover was too deep for our remaining piece of pole. We decided to moor the boat once we were in the clear. It was thirsty work and a drink at the Tostock Gardeners Arms went down well before we made for home.

I returned a couple of weeks later to the lake, as I was concerned about the outcome of the nest owing to the unexpected delay that night. It was a relief to see seven young ducklings swimming with their mum.

* * *

I didn't have the cheek to write to the Angling Club Secretary, saying that now the punt was being repainted it would also need a new pole.

Skomer Island

Every year in May my family and I would go on a week's holiday during the height of the breeding season in the hope of extending my photographic collection of nests and eggs of different species.   One of our favourite places was Pembrokeshire in Wales; we were always lucky with the weather and it rarely rained.

During our time there I always liked to spend a day on Skomer Isle; my wife and son preferred to relax on the caravan site where we were based. Skomer is one of the finest islands for sea bird colonies in the country. Situated two miles off the coast, the departure point was Martin's Haven.

For anyone interested in sea birds this was the place to be. Apart from the many birds, multi-coloured rabbits could be seen running about. They were left many years ago when the island was inhabited for a short while. There is an excellent little book worth reading about Skomer, called "The Cliffs of Freedom", possibly obtainable from libraries.

I was furiously attacked by a Greater Black Backed Gull, when taking a photo of its nest. This also happened when walking into a colony of Lesser Back Backed Gulls. The Herring Gulls didn't bother me too much.

I accidentally stepped on a rabbit's burrow, which gave way under my foot. I put my arm down the hole expecting to retrieve a puffin, only to bring out a Manx Shearwater, which was incubating its single white egg. I replaced the bird, as it is strictly nocturnal, and then carried on.

There were multitudes of Kittiwakes, Razorbills and Guillemots happily incubating their eggs on the steep inaccessible cliff ledges, a wonderful sight! Waiting for the boat to take us back, I took photographs of the very friendly Puffins

Holidays come and go very quickly. Once home I felt that, as I already had pictures of three gulls, the Black Headed Gull would be an excellent addition. They were only to be found in numbers on nature reserves like Minsmere (there were none on Skomer).

I knew of a small inland breeding colony of about six pairs at Bury St. Edmunds sugar beet factory, on their sediment pits. I wrote for permission to bird-watch there. This time I did get a reply, but not the one I expected, 'Sorry, out of bounds to all but employees'. As you may have already guessed, off I went! On arriving, all the gulls, what few there were, objected to my presence flying and squawking, telling all and sundry I was there. The nearest nest was about thirty feet from the bank. I thought I would walk on the crusty surface to the nest, take my photo then make a swift exit. How wrong I was!

I went down the grassy bank and my first step on the surface found me up to my thighs in thick black silt. Trying not to panic, I clasped a grass tussock and eventually getting to safety. I was helluva mucky, but safe! It had looked perfectly straightforward at the start. The outcome could have been very much worse. Obviously, I didn't get my photographs.

A couple of years later I did get my Black Headed Gull photographs at the largest colony in the country: Ravenglass Bird Reserve in Cumbria. I obtained a permit from the Carlisle Courts to enter the reserve. They kindly put up a hide for me, six feet from a nest, to photograph the sitting bird. Lovely photographs were taken.

The reserve warden, an elderly gentleman, escorted me through the many nests, leaving me in the hide. His name was Mr. Skeels.

Black Headed Gull on nest

The estimated number of breeding pairs at that time was 10-15,000, situated in the Drigg sand dunes belonging to the Muncaster Estate. I was exceptionally lucky to get a permit. They explained that no one normally was allowed in the reserve during the nesting season.

The Nightjar

Every year the Forestry Commission cut down large areas of mature woodland; once the ground is reasonably cleared, it is then replanted with seedlings.

The area I shall write about is a place I regularly visited during the summer months, often with my family, at weekends. It was a nice walk down the forest rides from Thetford Warren where I parked my car. Permits to enter the forests themselves were withdrawn at that time.

This young forest, about five or six years of age, had lots of bare ground strewn with bark that had been left from the previous felling, with very little vegetation apart from fine grasses. It was a perfect habitat for my favourite bird, the Nightjar.

I see young forests today of the same age with masses of mixed grasses and bracken up to the first branches of the trees with no bare areas. This is totally unsuitable nesting ground for the Nightjar. It is all to do with modern farming methods, I think. Our Nightjar is the only bird of its species to appear in this country – there are seventy-five worldwide. They arrive here from Africa about the middle of May, departing in August. In those three months they hope to rear two broods; it is indeed a very short period.

The Nightjar is strictly nocturnal, about the size of a Blackbird, with long wings and tail, and lovely soft plumage likened to that of Owls. It nests on the bare ground (there is no structured nest), laying only two eggs. They are renowned to be the most beautiful of all British birds' eggs that is why they are much sought after by egg collectors.

The best time to find their eggs is the first week in June. By that time the whole population will have laid. It's strange that a strictly nocturnal bird prefers to nest in the open, sometimes in partial shade of a small tree. There were thirteen pairs occupying the area in question.

The incubating birds rely on their plumage for camouflage, which blends so well with the remnants of bark left from the previous trees. They will not take flight even if you approach within a foot. (See photograph face-to-face with sitting bird whilst lying 6 feet away). Both male and female birds incubate, although I have never flushed a male off the eggs. One cannot mistake the male bird as he alone has white mirrors in his primary (wing) and tail feathers. The non-incubating bird is almost impossible to find during the day, as it will be resting on some branch, sitting lengthways not across like all other birds. Perhaps this is because it has short, weak legs. I have, by chance, a photograph of one sitting on a tree stump, and another taken from my car while having a picnic at Lakenheath Warren, as it sat on a red battered five-gallon drum, a most unusual perch.

I go to listen at night to the churring males then search by day for their nests. They become active from twilight onwards and, having large eyes and mouth, are well equipped for catching night-flying insects, moths, beetles and cockchafers.

The Nightjar has a most unusual feature. Their middle claw is pectinated (comb-like), for what purpose this is used has never been explained. Perhaps I can throw some light on this extraordinary feature at the end of this story.

One Sunday afternoon I had just flushed a Nightjar off its eggs when I disturbed a Red Deer stag. It looked as large as an elegant cow with massive antlers. It went stampeding towards where my wife was sunning herself on nearby grass. Luckily it missed her but gave her quite a fright – it could have been nasty.

I asked her to come and see the Nightjar eggs that I had found only minutes before. When we got there one had already hatched in that short time. The young bird was so camouflaged that you could hardly see it (see picture).

As these birds are here for only a short period, it seems they cut corners in their breeding habits. The incubating time is eighteen days and the fledging period about the same. When the chicks from the first brood are about nine days old, the male bird takes charge of them while his mate lays for the second time.

When searching for their eggs, one has to keep an eye out for adders. They both share the same habitat. Adders are lovely creatures and not a problem if left alone.

One evening I heard six churring male birds in another area where the trees were only about a foot high. The following morning, armed with a light telescopic fishing rod (ideal implement for covering a lot of ground), I systematically searched this entire young plantation. I did not put up a single bird, only a multitude of insects.

If the Nightjars are successful in rearing their young, they will return the following year to lay their eggs in the same spot. The only other bird to do this is the Stone Curlew.

I have at times taken friends to see and hear the Nightjars, stopping first for a drink at the Grafton Arms public house at Barham near Thetford before continuing on, arriving about 9.15 pm (churring starts about 9.45). I remember once taking two ladies; one was the deputy head and the other a teacher

Nightjar on stump

Nightjar chick just hatched

Nightjar on the drum

Face to face

from the school where I too was a teacher. I can picture them both lying on the grass with their jumpers over their heads protecting themselves from the numerous insects prior to the Nightjar becoming active. They were well rewarded when the birds were flying only yards above their heads making their lovely 'kooick' sounds.

Being in the heart of the Breckland at night is an experience not to be forgotten, a completely different world. With all the different sounds, you are never alone, the lovely churring of the Nightjar, the Reeling Grasshopper Warbler, Long Eared Owl cooing rather than hooting, and the eerie wailing of the Stone Curlew, not forgetting the barking of foxes and deer.

Possible Explanation of Pectinated Claw

I bought a small book from a second-hand bookshop many years ago called "Winged Life of the Tropics" printed in 1800. The story covering the Nightjar, or Goatsucker as they are often called, mentioned the pectinated claw. It was assumed that as their diet was mainly moths, beetles, cockchafers, etc. this claw was used for knocking off the hard wing casing of these creatures, which sounds a feasible explanation to me.

Orford Island

I knew Stowmarket had a freshwater angling club, whether they had a sea section I cannot say. I was chatting to a friend in the town who told me that a fishing party was going to fish the following Sunday on Orford Island for cod, whiting, etc., one of the more productive places on our coast. Orford Island starts at Slaughden (Aldeburgh), a shingle strip separated from the mainland by the River Alde, which runs into the North Sea at Shingle Street, 9 miles distant.

The Island can only be reached by boat crossing the Alde. The fishing club had a boat, as well as a few other boats not moored but upside-down beyond high water level at Boyton. It was arranged for me to go with them to bird watch for the day, dropping me off in the morning and picking me up late afternoon. An opportunity not to be missed. I had the Island to myself, just the birds and a few hares; this was before the National Trust took over. As usual my intention was to see what was breeding there and to photograph as many nests as possible. Most birds that nest on shingle don't, or hardly ever, have nesting material. Their eggs are laid on the bare shingle. A cold search for their eggs is definitely not recommended (just looking and hoping to find them) as the eggs or small young could easily be trodden on.

Ringed Plovers are found on the beaches all along our coast and they are quite common; here there were a few pairs, an ideal place for any nesting bird well away from beach-walkers. To the experienced these nests/eggs are easy to find once the birds themselves show you where they are. One nest of Oystercatchers took me longer to find than I expected. Two nests of Gulls were easily found, one of the Lesser Black-backed the other a Herring Gull. There was a garden-type shed (locked) where a pair of Shellducks was nesting underneath;

this nest held eight eggs. Shellduck invariably choose somewhere dark to nest: a rabbit burrow perhaps or under gorse bushes and such like. As with most ground-nesting birds: Plovers, Terns, Oystercatchers, Lapwings, etc., their young will not move when you approach. It is only when the parents feel that danger has passed will they tell them to move. One could accidentally stand on them first. I have always said that movement gives away their position.

Spot the two Little Tern eggs (answer at end of book)

My best find was a small colony (seven pairs) of Little Tern. They did not have the protection then that they have today, although on this Island they were quite safe. Little Terns don't nest in close proximity to one another like the Common Sandwich and other Terns. Their nests are several yards apart. When they return to their eggs they hover above before dropping down on to them. It was a good time for me to sit at a distance to have my snack and keep watch through binoculars, making a mental note of anything strange near their eggs, such as a large stone, perhaps a discarded bottle or can. There is usually something that helps to mark their position.

After relaxing for about half an hour, off I went in search of the eggs. When nearing the spot that I had mentally envisaged, it was time to get on my hands and knees for a fingertip search, going over the pebbles until the eggs were located. I found six sets of two eggs, the final seventh, to my surprise, had two-day old chicks, which were two feet apart. They also blended with the pebbles. For an example see the photograph of two eggs lying on the bare pebbles. The only other birds I came across were Skylark and Meadow Pipits in the areas of sparse vegetation. There was a colony of Common Terns on the extreme tip of the island, much too far for me to walk on that day. I had previously seen them from across the river at Shingle Street.

Spot Two Little Tern Chicks (answer at end)

When I arrived home, I related to my wife everything I had seen and what a wonderful day I had had, even the weather was kind. It's a good job it didn't rain. It was certainly a one-off.

***

I was told at a later date that several boats had been vandalised making them unseaworthy (what a senseless act).

A Shot in the Dark

A friend of a friend was told of a pair of Barn Owls feeding their young in an isolated oak tree situated in open countryside. My friend and I went to investigate. The entrance to this tree hollow was about seven feet high and awkward to reach but, with a little help, I managed to peer inside. There were many pellets and a Mallard Duck's nest from which the young had flown but no sign of Barn Owl chicks. I told my mate that we were too late and the young must have flown, but had they?

Owl sitting on nest in the oak tree,
unseen until the camera flash revealed.

The following year we returned, bringing with us a small pair of steps. I inspected this large cavity yet again, still no sign of the Owls. We returned to my car where we could look over the whole area. Within minutes along came an Owl carrying food. It went straight into the hole that we had only just inspected. Back we went, knowing they were in there somewhere. As I couldn't see any sign of a bird, I took a photograph using the flash (digital). I asked my mate to look at the result and sure enough there was the Owl sitting on eggs in the pitch darkness in a corner about four feet away.

Beside oak tree nest about to feed young.

Having permission from the owner, we went back a few times to photograph from a hide. On one visit the Owl, after feeding its four chicks, posed for me for over five minutes at the entrance hole, preening itself. How magical is that?

Unexpected Events

Golden Oriole

One sunny afternoon J.R. and I were walking through the woods at Thetford when we heard a wonderful melodious song in the distance, not knowing from which bird it came, as it was not familiar to us.

In the library at the school where I worked was a BBC long-playing record of bird songs. On playing this record, I came across the song we heard that day; it was the Golden Oriole. It was the first year it bred at no great distance from where we were. It is a very colourful summer visitor about the size of a Mistle Thrush. It bred in Norfolk for the first time in the 1870s in someone's garden. It had three young that were killed by a cat. One pair attempted to breed at Lowestoft several years ago, but the bird deserted its nest, which contained one egg, probably due to human disturbance.

Nest Boxes in Forest

Visiting young plantations was a regular thing during spring/summer months. One spring I noticed the appearance of a large number of nesting boxes. All were fixed to mature trees five or six feet high and spaced approximately forty yards apart.

I was told that a Dr. David Lack was carrying out some sort of experiment, birds versus insecticides. Being a nest-box enthusiast, I made a point of checking these boxes to see what was occupying them. As expected there were many Cole Tits, as these are the most numerous in coniferous woods, followed by Great Tits and Blue Tits. To my surprise, five boxes were taken by Common Redstarts; it must have been a very good year for them. One would be very fortunate to see the odd pair of these attractive birds a year.

Crossbill

My best years in the Breck were the 1960s/70s. From then on there were many more people roaming about, especially since the Forest Enterprise (offshoot of the Forestry Commission) allowed the public to enter the forest for leisure activities (not cars).

JR and I would start our year in January searching for the nests of the Crossbills, our earliest nesting bird. In fact, we proved that some pairs start nesting in early December, when we found a dead, fully fledged juvenile in the snow on the 19th January. At that time, during the 1960s, there were only six breeding sites known to us, all roadside in Scotch fir, and near human dwellings. The reason for their closeness to humans is that they are very thirsty birds. Most people had chickens that always had water, and the Crossbills took advantage of this.

Most nests were usually high up; one exception was only six feet on an overhanging roadside branch near the Elveden "Six Day Inn" on the Brandon Road.

Heron/Bittern

Twice I have been startled by long-legged birds (the feathered variety). It was quite usual for me on a Friday night, before going to the Tostock Gardeners Arms Public House, to go to my old haunt at Low Meadows. There I would listen to the calls of the marsh birds: Water Rails, Redshank, etc. Standing motionless in the twilight a Heron came down and stood right beside me. Within seconds, realising I was a human, it immediately took flight. I don't know who was the more startled.

***

The second time was early one sunny morning when looking for the nests of Bearded Tits in the reed beds at Walberswick. Standing motionless, again in a small clearing in the reeds, listening to the delightful "ping ping" calls of the Bearded Tits, I found I was not alone. After a couple of minutes a Bittern decided to take flight, which had been standing nearby unseen by me. Pheasant will often do this too; when they do, it can be quite startling.

Little Grebe

The time of year was the third week in April, my destination the Breckland meres. The objective was to find and photograph the nest and eggs of the Little Grebe. They bred on them all.

The meres I visited, mostly by myself, or with my family and sometimes with JR, were Ringmere, Langmere, Fowlmere (18 acres) and the Devil's Punchbowl. The first two are on the Norfolk Naturalist Trust's nature reserve at East Wretham. Water levels fluctuate a great deal; Ringmere can be dry while Langmere, a short distance away, can be full. All these Breckland meres teem with wildlife, or rather they did.

A Gadwall drake

I arrived at Ringmere at about quarter past eight, to see a small boat moored on the southern side. I had never seen a boat on any of these meres before so I couldn't understand why there should be on this occasion. However, it was very convenient. I used this boat to go out and photograph the Grebes' nest. This time I returned the boat to where I found it, not like the adventure I had as Drinkstone; the circumstances were a little different.

Of the many species of Duck encountered on these Breckland meres (eleven in all) I always associate the Gadwall Duck with the Breck. One pair of pinioned birds was introduced in 1850 and it's believed the population today stems from the successful breeding of that one pair.

Blackbird

A friend of mine, who was also a schoolboy chum when living in Tostock during the 1940s, now had a farm at Woolpit. A couple of years had passed since I covered a Kestrel nest on his property. He phoned me one day saying that he had a Blackbird nesting on the ground in the lea of a hedge. I told him that it was not too unusual for a Blackbird to do this. I went over to see him. A female Blackbird appeared to be sitting on the ground. After flushing her from where she sat, I could see three eggs in a dry bare scrape – now that is a sight I had never seen before.

The unfortunate thing was that within a week the hedge was trimmed exposing the eggs. Naturally, the eggs were deserted. I'm surprised the birds decided to lay their eggs without a proper nest; they can build one within three/four days.

Woodlark

Thetford Warren was a haven for many breeding birds. The Woodlark was just one of them, but they were not plentiful. For some unknown reason they disappeared from the Warren altogether.

It was probably the following spring, when my family and I were walking down a ride between the forests. There had been an April shower and the sun was now shining when my wife heard the unmistakable song of the Woodlark. We found that there were six pairs nesting on the grass-bordered young forest. When Woodlark ascend, singing as they do so, they fly in circles, but Skylark fly straight.

We assume these Woodlark were the ones that had vanished from the Warren.

Golden Pheasants

Golden Pheasant

Walking eastwards down a track (not ride) on Thetford Warren, a male Golden Pheasant crossed ahead of us, followed at regular intervals of about ten seconds by four more (five in all). It was like an action replay; they were all males.

The males have striking colours and we only used to see the odd bird, mostly around the Santon Downham area, so this was a rare occurrence.

Kestrel at Lakenheath Warren

On one of our weekend excursions in the Breck, we parked on Lakenheath Warren for a picnic. We often found it an advantage to remain in the car as birds accept this and carry on doing what they do. After a bite to eat, my son, Adrian, went walkabout nearby and like his father always on the lookout for something. Suddenly, a male Kestrel came down and landed in the bracken just a few yards from him. He immediately froze. I got out of the car with my camera and walking towards him, using him as a shield. I took several photographs from over his shoulder before the bird flew off. I wouldn't say it was an escapee as there was no sign of jesses.

Cavenham

The first week in June saw me searching for birds' nests at a lovely habitat at Cavenham near Icklingham. Sparsely spaced hawthorn bushes and young saplings with the River Lark not far away, this was an ideal habitat for the Red-backed Shrike and the tiny Lesser Redpoll. I often find these two birds in the same area.

I came across what I thought was a Red-backed Shrike's nest that was up about seven to eight feet high. I thought at the time that it was rather high for this species. I climbed to this nest to find it was of a Yellow Bunting, the highest nest I have ever seen for this bird.

I must admit the nests of these two birds are very similar in appearance.

The Sparrow Hawk

We all like to see birds in our gardens. To encourage them we put up feeders, fat balls, nuts, seeds, and the favourite: sunflower hearts.

During the summer months there is plenty of natural food, but it is in the autumn/winter period when more birds will visit your feeders. There is often a lull period when the regular feeding birds go to other gardens, possibly for a change of diet.

The other alternative to these quiet times is the presence of the Sparrow Hawk. You feed and encourage the birds but this, in turn, draws the attention of this attractive bird of prey, so you only have yourself to blame for any casualties. I know some people who don't feed the birds for this reason. Many who feed the birds dislike this Hawk coming into their gardens and catching the odd bird. The Collared Dove is one of their favourites. I must admit they are not the most humane killers as they pluck and tear off pieces of flesh until the victim is dead. I have watched this often even though I am not a bloodthirsty person, but try not to interfere with Nature. It is said Nature is cruel and it certainly is.

On occasions during the winter months I put up my hide about seven feet from my feeding station and, once settled in, it is pot luck from then on. The regular Great Spotted Woodpecker, Long Tailed, Great, Blue, Cole and Marsh Tits visit, together with other common birds.

During one of the aforementioned quiet periods, sitting right in front of me was the Sparrow Hawk (pictured), which stayed for several minutes.

Sparrow Hawk

Previous photographs of this bird were taken through my kitchen window but not of the quality I now have. It was certainly a red-letter day for me.

The male Sparrow Hawk is one of our smallest raptors recognised by his orange eyes, the female has yellow eyes. As with all birds of prey, the females are the larger of the two; the female Sparrow Hawk is almost twice the weight of her mate, and both are incredibly fast on the wing. During the late 1950s they almost disappeared owing to the use of insecticides: D.D.T., Aldrin, etc. but with the ban on these chemicals I'm glad to say they are once again widespread.

Believe this or Not

Travelling from Orford towards Tunstall forests on a Sunday afternoon, I saw, no not a UFO, something much rarer, a manure heap smothered with Hooded Crows; we call them Hoodies.

Amazed at the sight I immediately braked, not thinking of the driver following me, who sounded his horn in annoyance startling the Crows, which then flew and settled way down on the ploughed field. Through my binoculars I counted twenty-six. By the time I got out of my car to take a photograph, a woman appeared with her dog and all but two of the Hoodies flew away but they were too far away for me to take any useful pictures.

I have never seen more than two Hoodies in any winter, sometimes none at all. Hooded Crows come down here from the north of England and are mostly seen on our tidal rivers, the River Orwell being one.

At that time I used to send bird sightings to the Suffolk Naturalist Society for their annual 'Bird Report', but this was not accepted by the committee, nor was an estimated count of 300 Waxwings feeding on hawthorn at Eastbridge. I don't suppose you believe this either. I'm not in the habit of writing what I only imagine I see

I hope this book has served as an encouragement to readers to sample for themselves the attractions of birdwatching in the various habitats that East Anglia can provide. Much enjoyment can be derived from the peace and quiet of countryside as an antidote to the busy technical world we live in today.

Position of Little Tern eggs

Position of Little Tern Chicks